Oracle RMAN
Pocket Reference

Oracle RMAN
Pocket Reference

Darl Kuhn and Scott Schulze

Beijing · Cambridge · Farnham · Köln · Paris · Sebastopol · Taipei · Tokyo

Oracle RMAN Pocket Reference
by Darl Kuhn and Scott Schulze

Copyright © 2002 O'Reilly & Associates, Inc. All rights reserved.
Printed in the United States of America.

Published by O'Reilly & Associates, Inc.,
1005 Gravenstein Highway North, Sebastopol, CA 95472.

O'Reilly & Associates books may be purchased for educational,
business, or sales promotional use. Online editions are also available for
most titles (*safari.oreilly.com*). For more information contact our
corporate/institutional sales department: (800) 998-9938 or
corporate@oreilly.com.

Editor:	Jonathan Gennick
Production Editor:	Matt Hutchinson
Cover Designer:	Pam Spremulli
Interior Designer:	David Futato

Printing History:

January 2002:	First Edition

0-596-00233-5
[C]

Contents

Oracle RMAN
Pocket Reference

Introduction

This book is a quick-reference guide for Recovery Manager (RMAN), Oracle's utility to manage all of your Oracle database backup and recovery activities. This book is not a comprehensive backup and recovery book. It contains an overview of RMAN architecture, shows briefly how to backup and restore databases using RMAN, describes catalog setup issues, and provides quick-reference syntax diagrams of RMAN commands.

The purpose of this book is to help you quickly find the syntax for, and use, RMAN commands to back up, restore, and recover a database. We assume that you, the reader, have basic Oracle database administrator (DBA) skills, and that you are familiar with backup and recovery concepts. We also point out that the batch mode examples in this book are scripted with Unix shell scripts. Many of these examples contain Unix paths that are appropriate for our environment. If you are developing your own set of scripts, you will want to change the examples to reflect your own environment.

Acknowledgments

Many thanks to "our man," editor Jonathan Gennick. His feedback and suggestions have added significant improvements and clarity to this book. Thanks also to the technical reviewers Jeff Cox, Tim Gorman, Dick Goulet, Mark Hampton, Steve Orr, Walt Weaver, and Jeremiah Wilton.

Caveats

We have taken the Pareto's Law approach in writing this book, in that we have tried to cover topics that you are most likely to encounter while using RMAN. This material does not cover every type of environment, nor does it cover all of the backup and recovery scenarios that you will encounter as an Oracle DBA.

While some of the more common backup and recovery scenarios are covered in this book, it is still critical that you are comfortable with your RMAN implementation and can recover your database no matter what type of failure occurs. We can't stress enough the importance of regular testing in preparation for recovering from unplanned disasters.

A sound implementation and regular testing will give you the confidence to handle the impending 2 A.M. call: "Hey, I'm getting this strange ORA-01116 error, unable to open file, what do I do?"

Conventions

UPPERCASE
> Indicates an RMAN keyword, SQL keyword, or the name of a database object.

italic
> Used for filenames, directory names, and URLs. Also used for emphasis and for the first use of a technical term.

Constant width
> Used for examples showing code.

Constant width bold
> Indicates user input in examples showing an interaction.

Constant width italic
> Used in syntax descriptions to indicate user-defined terms.

[]   Used in syntax descriptions to denote optional elements.

{}   Used in syntax descriptions to denote a required choice.

| Used in syntax descriptions to separate choices.

_   Used in syntax descriptions to indicate that the underlined option is the default.

O/S
> Abbreviation of "operating system."

RMAN Architecture

Recovery Manager (RMAN) is a utility that can manage all of your Oracle backup and recovery activities. DBAs are often wary of using RMAN because of its perceived complexity and its control over performing critical tasks. The traditional backup and recovery methods are tried-and-true. Thus, when your livelihood depends on your ability to back up and recover the database, why implement a technology like RMAN? The reason is that RMAN comes with several benefits:

- Incremental backups that only copy data blocks that have changed since the last backup.
- Tablespaces are not put in *backup* mode, thus there is no extra redo log generation during online backups.
- Detection of corrupt blocks during backups.
- Parallelization of I/O operations.
- Automatic logging of all backup and recovery operations.
- Built-in reporting and listing commands.

RMAN's architecture is a combination of an executable program (the *rman* utility) and background processes that interact with one or more databases and with I/O devices. There are several key architectural components to be aware of:

- RMAN executable
- Server processes
- Channels
- Target database
- Recovery catalog database (optional)
- Media management layer (optional)
- Backups, backup sets, and backup pieces

The following sections describe each of these components.

RMAN Executable

The RMAN executable, usually named *rman,* is the program that manages all backup and recovery operations. You interact with the RMAN executable to specify backup and recovery operations you want to perform.

NOTE

You don't need an extra license for RMAN; it comes as a standard utility included with an Oracle 8.0.x, Oracle8*i,* or Oracle9*i* installation.

The executable then interacts with the target database, starts the necessary server processes, and performs the operations that you requested. Finally, the RMAN executable records those operations in the target database's control file and the recovery catalog database, if you have one.

Server Processes

RMAN *server processes* are background processes, started on the server, used to communicate between RMAN and the databases. They can also communicate between RMAN and any disk, tape, or other I/O devices. RMAN server processes

---

do all the real work for a backup or restore operation, and a typical backup or restore operation results in several server processes being started.

Server processes are started under the following conditions:

- When you start RMAN and connect to your target database
- When you connect to your catalog—if you are using a recovery catalog database
- When you allocate and open an I/O channel during a backup or recovery operation

Channels

A *channel* is an RMAN server process started when there is a need to communicate with an I/O device, such as a disk or a tape. A channel is what reads and writes RMAN backup files. Any time you issue an RMAN *allocate channel* command, a server process is started on the target database server. It is through the allocation of channels that you govern I/O characteristics such as:

- Type of I/O device being read or written to, either a disk or an sbt_tape
- Number of processes simultaneously accessing an I/O device
- Maximum size of files created on I/O devices
- Maximum rate at which database files are read
- Maximum number of files open at a time

Target Database

The *target database* is the database on which RMAN performs backup, restore, and recovery operations. This is the database that owns the datafiles, control files, and archived redo files that are backed up, restored, or recovered. Note that RMAN does not back up the online redo logs of the target database.

Recovery Catalog Database

The *recovery catalog database* is an optional repository used by RMAN to record information concerning backup and recovery activities performed on the target. The recovery catalog consists of three components:

- A separate database referred to as the catalog database (from the target database)
- A schema within the catalog database
- Tables (and supporting objects) within the schema that contain data pertaining to RMAN backup and recovery operations performed on the target

The catalog is typically a database that you build on a different host from your target database. The reason for this is that you don't want a failure on the target host to affect your ability to use the catalog. If both the catalog and target are on the same box, a single media failure can put you in a situation from which you can't recover your target database.

Inside the catalog database is a special schema containing the tables that store information about RMAN backup and recovery activities. This includes information such as:

- Details about the physical structure of the target database
- A log of backup operations performed on the target database's datafiles, control files, and archived redo log files
- Stored scripts containing frequently used sequences of RMAN commands

Why is the catalog optional? When RMAN performs any backup operation, it writes information about that task to the target database's control files. Therefore, RMAN does not need a catalog to operate. If you choose to implement a recovery catalog database, then RMAN will store additional information about what was backed up—often called *metadata*—in the catalog.

NOTE

A common misconception is that the catalog stores the physical backup files for the target database. The catalog contains only information about the backups of the target database—not the physical backup files themselves.

The primary reason for implementing a catalog is that it enables the greatest flexibility in backup and recovery scenarios. Using a catalog gives you access to a longer history of backups and allows you to manage all of your backup and recovery operations from one repository. Utilizing a catalog makes available to you all the features of RMAN. For reasons such as these, we recommend using a catalog database.

NOTE

The recovery catalog database is frequently referred to simply as the *catalog* or the *catalog database*. We use both terms throughout this book.

Media Management Layer

The *Media Management Layer* (MML) is a third-party piece of software that manages the reading and writing of files to and from tape. An MML also keeps track of which files have been written to which tapes. If you want to back up your database files to tape, RMAN requires you to use an MML. If you plan to use RMAN to back up files only to disk, you do not need an MML.

MML tools are often used by System Administrators to back up the host O/S filesystems. If your work environment already uses a MML, you can leverage this architecture to implement RMAN backups to tape. There are several reasons to back up files to tape and thus require an MML:

- The expense of storing large backups on disk is too costly.
- Your requirement is to back up files somewhere other than on the same server as the target database, thus reducing your risk of losing both the target database and backup files at the same time

When backing up files to tape, an MML keeps track of which files were written to which tapes. In the event that restoration of a database file is required, RMAN communicates to the MML a list of the backup files that are required to restore the database file. The MML then determines which tapes contain the required backup files, retrieves the requested backup files, and passes them back to RMAN; RMAN then restores the database file.

Setting up RMAN to work with an MML can be the most frustrating and difficult part of implementing RMAN. This is because determining the root cause of an issue can be problematic when multiple software vendors are involved.

Backups, Backup Sets, and Backup Pieces

When you issue an RMAN *backup* command, RMAN creates *backup sets*, which are logical groupings of physical files. The physical files that RMAN creates on your backup media are called *backup pieces*. When working with RMAN, you need to understand that the following terms have specific meanings:

RMAN backup
    A backup of all or part of your database. This results from issuing an RMAN *backup* command. A backup consists of one or more backup sets.

Backup set

A logical grouping of backup files—the backup pieces—that are created when you issue an RMAN *backup* command. A backup set is RMAN's name for a collection of files associated with a backup. A backup set is composed of one or more backup pieces.

Backup piece

A physical binary file created by RMAN during a backup. Backup pieces are written to your backup medium, whether to disk or tape. They contain blocks from the target database's datafiles, archived redo log files, and control files.

When RMAN constructs a backup piece from datafiles, there are a several rules that it follows:

- A datafile cannot span backup sets.
- A datafile can span backup pieces as long as it stays within one backup set.
- Datafiles and control files can coexist in the same backup sets.
- Archived redo log files are never in the same backup set as datafiles or control files.

RMAN is the only tool that can operate on backup pieces. If you need to restore a file from an RMAN backup, you must use RMAN to do it. There's no way for you to manually reconstruct database files from the backup pieces. You must use RMAN to restore files from a backup piece.

Starting RMAN

This section explains some of the prerequisites that must be in place before you can use RMAN. It then shows you how to invoke RMAN and finally, how to connect to a target database both with and without using a recovery catalog.

Target Prerequisites

If you already have your target database environment set up, you can skip this section. If not, there are a few things you need to have in place before instructing RMAN to connect to the target:

- Appropriate target environment variables must be established.
- You must have access to an O/S account or a schema that has SYSDBA privileges.

Before you connect to your target database, you must ensure that the standard Unix environment variables are established. These variables include: ORACLE_SID, ORACLE_HOME, PATH, NLS_LANG, and NLS_DATE_FORMAT. They govern the name of the instance, the path to the RMAN executable; and the behavior of backup, restore, and reporting commands.

NOTE

When using RMAN, NLS_LANG should be set to the character set that your database was created with. If you do not set NLS_LANG, you may encounter problems when issuing BACKUP, RESTORE, and RECOVER commands.

Once you have the appropriate environment variables set, you then need access to an O/S account or a database schema that has SYSDBA privileges. You must have access to the SYSDBA privilege before you can connect to the target database using RMAN. There are two methods of administering the SYSDBA privilege:

- Locally via O/S authentication
- Remotely via password file

O/S authentication is established when you install the Oracle binaries. At that time, you set up a Unix group, often named *dba*, and specify this as the O/S group with SYSDBA privileges. Often the Unix account used to install the Oracle binaries is named *oracle*. This account is usually set up to belong to the *dba* group, and consequently, it lets you start RMAN and connect to the target database.

NOTE

O/S authentication is what permits you to connect locally without having to specify the *AS* SYSDBA option. For local connections, RMAN automatically connects you to the target database with SYSDBA privileges.

Setting up a password file is the other method by which you can administer the SYSDBA privilege. There are two good reasons to use RMAN with a password file:

- Oracle has deprecated the use of CONNECT INTERNAL and Server Manager.
- You may want to administer RMAN remotely through a network connection.

For example, if you're in an environment where you want to back up all of your target databases from one place and not have to log on to each host and back up the database, you must do it via a network connection. To remotely administer RMAN through a network connection, you need to do the following:

- Create a password file
- Enable remote logins for password file users

To create the password file, as the Oracle software owner or as a member of the *dba* group, *cd* to the *$ORACLE_HOME/ dbs* directory, and issue the *orapwd* command:

```
$ orapwd file=orapwsidname password=password entries=n
```

There are three user-provided variables in this example:

sidname
    The SID of the target instance

password
    The password to be used when you connect a user SYS
    with SYSDBA privilege

n   The maximum number of schemas allowed in the pass-
    word files.

For example, say that you have an instance named *brdstn*,
that you want the password to be *patni*, and that you want at
the most 30 entries in the password file:

```
$ cd $ORACLE_HOME/dbs
```

```
$ orapwd file=orapwbrdstn password=patni entries=30
```

The resulting password file is named *orapwdbrdstn* and is in
the *$ORACLE_HOME/dbs* directory.

After you create a password file, you need to enable remote
logins. To do this, set the instance's REMOTE_LOGIN_
PASSWORDFILE initialization parameter to exclusive, as
shown:

```
remote_login_passwordfile = exclusive
```

Setting this parameter to exclusive signifies that only one
database can use the password file and that users other than
sys and *internal* can reside in it. You can now use a network
connection to connect to your target database as SYSDBA.

Note that you have to create a password file only for the target database and not for the catalog. This is because when
you connect to the target, you need to connect as an account
that has the SYSDBA privilege. When you connect remotely
to a target database, the SYSDBA privilege is enabled
through the password file. This is unlike a connection to the
catalog, for which SYSDBA is not required, because you log
in as the owner of the catalog schema.

When the SYSDBA privilege is granted to a specified user, that user can be queried in the V$PWFILE_USERS view. For example:

```
SQL> grant SYSDBA to rmanadmin;

Grant succeeded.

SQL> select * from v$pwfile_users where
     username='RMANADMIN';

USERNAME                        SYSDB SYSOP
------------------------------- ----- -----
RMANADMIN                       TRUE  FALSE
```

Invoking the RMAN Executable

In order to use RMAN, you have to invoke the executable. Once you've invoked the executable, you get an RMAN prompt, from which you can execute RMAN commands. The executable for RMAN is located with all of the other Oracle executables, in the *bin* directory of your Oracle installation.

NOTE

The examples in this section assume that you're in a Unix environment and have access to the *oracle* Unix O/S account.

To invoke the RMAN executable, issue the *rman* command from your O/S command prompt. You are presented with an RMAN prompt:

```
$ rman

Recovery Manager: Release 9.0.1.0.0 - Production

RMAN>
```

From here you can use RMAN's command-line interface language to perform backup and recovery tasks.

Use the *exit* command to terminate the RMAN executable and return to your O/S command prompt:

```
RMAN> exit

$
```

The various command-line choices that are available are described in detail in the section "Command-Line Syntax" later in this book.

Connecting to a Target with No Catalog

The simplest way to use RMAN is to connect to a target database without a recovery catalog. You do this using the *nocatalog* command-line option.

O/S authentication

If you want to connect to a target database using O/S authentication, use the following command:

```
$ rman target / nocatalog

Recovery Manager: Release 9.0.1.0.0 - Production
connected to target database: BRDSTN (DBID=664610428)
using target database controlfile instead of recovery
catalog
```

You can use O/S authentication only from an O/S account on the database server.

NOTE

With Oracle 8.0.x and Oracle8i, you must specify *nocatalog* on the command line to connect without using a catalog. With Oracle9i, *nocatalog* is the default connection mode.

Password file authentication

If you are connecting to the target database via a network connection, you need to use a connect string. For this to work, you should have a password file in place for your target database. The following example connects to the target using the *sys* account with a password of *mooft*:

```
$ rman target / sys/mooft@brdstn nocatalog

Recovery Manager: Release 9.0.1.0.0 - Production
connected to target database: BRDSTN (DBID=664610428)
using target database controlfile instead of recovery
catalog
```

In this example, brdstn is a net service name. Net service names are typically defined in the *tnsnames.ora* file.

Hiding the password

Supplying usernames and passwords on the command line is convenient. Unfortunately, this practice poses a serious security risk. With Unix, your command line may be visible to other users on the system via the *ps* command. For example:

```
$ ps -ef | grep rman
oracle 27681 21612  3 16:54:02 pts/5 0:03 rman target /
    sys/mooft
```

You can see in this example that the output from the *ps* command shows the entire *rman* command, including the username and password. That's not good! Fortunately, there is a way around having your password show up in the process status output. Don't specify connection information while at the O/S prompt, but connect after an RMAN session as been initiated. For example:

```
$ rman nocatalog
Recovery Manager: Release 9.0.1.0.0 - Production

RMAN> connect target / sys/mooft@brdstn
```

```
connected to target database: BRDSTN (DBID=664610428)
using target database controlfile instead of recovery
catalog
```

Connecting to the database after RMAN has been invoked prevents any password information from showing up in a process list.

Connecting to Both a Target and a Catalog

If you're using a catalog, you will typically connect to the target and the catalog at the same time. This is because when you're performing backup and recovery operations both the target and the catalog need to be aware of your activities.

If you're logged on to the target database host, your connection to the catalog usually will be through a network connection. This is because in a production environment your catalog database should never reside on the same host as your target database. If your target and catalog are on the same host, you have a single point of failure, and you may not be able to recover your target database.

O/S authentication

The following example assumes you're logged onto the target host as the *oracle* user or a member of the *dba* group, and that a recovery catalog is in place. See the "Implementing a Catalog" section for more details on configuring a recovery catalog.

```
$ rman target / catalog rmancat/sholay@brdstnrc

Recovery Manager: Release 9.0.1.0.0 - Production

connected to target database: BRDSTN (DBID=664610428)

connected to recovery catalog database
```

This connects you to the target and catalog database at the same time. Alternatively, you can invoke RMAN first and then issue *connect* commands for the target and catalog, respectively:

```
$ rman

Recovery Manager: Release 9.0.1.0.0 - Production

RMAN> connect catalog rmancat/sholay@brdstnrc

connected to recovery catalog database

RMAN> connect target /

connected to target database: BRDSTN (DBID=3662736385)
```

Issuing *connect* commands from within RMAN prevents any passwords from appearing in the process list where other O/S users can view them.

Password authentication

If you are using a password file, the network connection to the target is made as shown in the following example. Note the use of a net service name for both connections.

```
$ rman

Recovery Manager: Release 9.0.1.0.0 - Production

RMAN> connect target / sys/namstay@brdstn

RMAN-06005: connected to target database: BRDSTN
(DBID=3662736385)

RMAN> connect catalog rmancat/sholay@brdstnrc

RMAN-06008: connected to recovery catalog database
```

It doesn't matter whether you connect to the target or the catalog first, as long as you connect to both before issuing any other RMAN commands.

Executing Commands

In order to perform any type of function from within RMAN, you must use the RMAN command syntax. An extensive array of commands is available, and you will often execute a series of commands to perform a task. You can issue commands either by typing them in at the RMAN prompt or by executing them from within O/S scripts or RMAN scripts.

Executing RMAN Commands from the RMAN Prompt

The most basic way of executing RMAN commands is to type them in manually from the RMAN command-line prompt. In fact, we recommend that you become familiar with this method. There are two good reasons for learning how to type in commands manually:

- Concepts are reenforced.
- It may be the only option available during a backup and recovery scenario.

In other words, don't rely on a tool for backup and recovery if you don't understand the underlying command syntax. You don't want to be caught in a situation in which you're responsible for a recovery but do not know how to compose ad hoc RMAN commands. Here's a simple example of how to do a full disk-based backup of datafiles by typing in the commands manually:

```
$ rman nocatalog

Recovery Manager: Release 9.0.1.0.0 - Production

RMAN> connect target /

connected to target database: BRDSTN (DBID=3662736385)
using target database controlfile instead of recovery
catalog
```

```
RMAN> run {allocate channel d1 type disk;
2> backup full format '/ora01/backup/rman_%d_%U.bus'
3> database;}
```

This performs a full database backup of datafiles to a local disk in the *ora01/backup* directory.

The target must be in *archivelog* mode before running an on-line backup. Here's an example of how to alter a database into *archivelog* mode:

```
SQL> connect sys/heeraa as sysdba;
SQL> alter database archivelog;
```

Even when simple tasks complete successfully, RMAN presents you with a voluminous information stack. When typing in commands manually, you have probably noticed that RMAN parses each line as you type it in. Therefore, if you type in something that is not syntactically correct, you are immediately presented with an error stack and must start over. The following example has a syntactical error on the second line. As soon as you type it and hit Return, RMAN displays an error stack:

```
RMAN> run {allocate channel d1 type disk;
2> backup full format '/ora01/backup/rman_%t.bus'

RMAN-00571:
===========================================
RMAN-00569: === ERROR MESSAGE STACK FOLLOWS ====
RMAN-00571:
===========================================
RMAN-00579: the following error occurred at 06/10/2001
13:08:39
RMAN-00558: error encountered while parsing input commands
RMAN-01005: syntax error: found "identifier": expecting
one of: "archivelog, backup, backupset, channel, check,
copies, controlfilecopy, cumulative, current, database,
datafile, datafilecopy, device, diskratio, filesperset,
format, full, force, incremental, keep, (, maxsetsize,
nochecksum, noexclude, nokeep, not, parm, proxy, pool,
skip, setsize, tablespace, tag, validate"
RMAN-01008: the bad identifier was: ful
RMAN-01007: at line 2 column 8 file: standard input
```

In other words, once you make a mistake, you have to figure out what you typed in that RMAN didn't like and then retype the command.

NOTE

In general, when running RMAN commands, if you don't see an RMAN-00569: === ERROR MESSAGE STACK FOLLOWS === message in the output, your command completed successfully.

Executing RMAN Commands from a File

This section explains how to run RMAN commands that you've stored in an O/S file. By executing commands from an O/S file, you promote code reusability, which makes it simpler to run commands in batch mode.

To run RMAN commands from a command file:

1. Put the commands in a text file.
2. Instruct RMAN to run the commands.

First, open up a file with your favorite text editor (such as *vi*) and enter the RMAN commands. The commands should be identical to what you would otherwise type in manually. For example, create a file called *full_back.rmn*, and place in it the following text. Note that for this example to work you must have a directory called */ora01/backup*.

```
# This script takes a full backup of the database.
run {
  # allocate a channel
  allocate channel d1 type disk;
  # issue the backup command
  backup full format '/ora01/backup/rman_%d_%U.bus'
    database;
}
```

To run the script, issue the following RMAN command to
connect to the target and catalog databases, and execute your
script:

```
$ rman target / nocatalog @full_back.rmn log=full_back.log
```

After your script completes, you can view the contents of
full_back.log to see if the job ran successfully.

Another way to run commands in an O/S file is to specify the
file after you've started RMAN:

```
$ rman nocatalog

RMAN> connect target /

RMAN> @full_back.rmn
```

Placing RMAN commands within O/S files offers a flexible
way to store and run your backup and recovery scripts. As
you design a backup and recovery strategy, you'll probably
create stored O/S scripts to automate common tasks.

Running SQL and O/S Commands from Within RMAN

Sometimes you may want to run an SQL statement from
within RMAN. Use RMAN's *sql* command to do this. For
example:

```
RMAN> sql "alter system switch logfile";
```

If there are single quote marks in your SQL, you need to use
two single quote marks as shown in this next example:

```
RMAN> sql "alter database datafile
  ''/d0101/ordadta/brdstn/users_01.dbf'' offline";
```

You can also run O/S commands using a similar technique with the *host* command:

```
RMAN> host "ls";
```

Some SQL commands, such as ALTER DATABASE, are directly supported by RMAN. These can be executed directly from the RMAN command prompt, without using the *sql* command. For example:

```
RMAN> alter database mount;
```

Note that the complete syntax of the SQL ALTER DATA-BASE command is not supported from within RMAN. Refer to the "RMAN Command Reference" section for RMAN-supported ALTER DATABASE syntax.

Running RMAN from Shell Scripts

In a Unix environment, you will probably want to run your RMAN commands from a shell script. Backup tasks, for example, can be automated through a scheduling tool (such as *cron*) that can call a shell script containing RMAN commands.

Shell basics

Here's an example of how to call RMAN commands from a shell script:

```
#!/bin/ksh
#------------------------------------------------
export TARGET_CONN=sys/gober@brdstn
export CATALOG_CONN=rman_cat_owner/gando@rman_cat
#------------------------------------------------
rman <<EOF
# Connect to the target and the catalog
connect target ${TARGET_CONN}
connect catalog ${CATALOG_CONN}
# Run the backup command.
        run { allocate channel d1 type disk;
            backup full format
                '/d0102/backup/rman_%U.bus' database; }
```

```
EOF
#
exit
```

There are several things to note about this example. Notice that two variables, TARGET_CONN and CATALOG_CONN, are used to hold the connection information. These variables are used as the connection strings after RMAN has been called within the script. This keeps the password from being visible in the process list.

The EOF text strings act as markers that tell Unix that any commands between the EOFs are commands associated with the command to the immediate left of the `` characters. While the EOF can be any text string, we'll use the EOF text as a standard in our shell script examples throughout this book.

If RMAN encounters an error, it returns a nonzero exit code that can be evaluated within the O/S shell script. For example:

```
... #Test for success of RMAN operation
if [ $? -ne 0 ]; then
# notify adminstrator of problem
fi
```

Before you run a shell script, ensure that the correct file permissions have been set so that the file is executable and does not have world-read permissions. Do this using the Unix *chmod* command:

```
$ chmod 750 filename
```

The 750 in this command ensures that the script file is executable and that only people in the same group as the owner of the file have read access to it.

Passing parameters to RMAN

With backup and recovery strategies, the key is to keep things as simple as possible. One way to reduce complexity is to pass parameters to your scripts. This technique promotes the reuse of code for similar tasks. One place where you may want to reuse code is with incremental RMAN backups. For example, you can use one script to handle all your incremental backups, passing the backup level as a parameter. One method for passing parameters to RMAN is to create a shell script and use shell variables for the RMAN commands you want to be dynamic. Here's an example of a shell script to which you pass the increment level and the destination directory for backup pieces:

```ksh
#!/bin/ksh
#----------------------------------------------
# Either hard code the next 3 variables or
# source them with an oraenv file.
export ORACLE_HOME=/ora01/app/oracle/product/8.1.6
export ORACLE_SID=brdstn
export PATH=$PATH:$ORACLE_HOME/bin
#----------------------------------------------
export MAILX="/usr/ucb/Mail"
export MAIL_LIST="aadamee@yahoo.com"
#----------------------------------------------
export BOX=`uname -a | awk '{print$2}'`
export PRG=`basename $0`
export USAGE="Usage: ${PRG} <level of incremental>-
<directory for backup piece>"
export RLEV=$1
export RDIR=$2
if [ -z "${RLEV}" -o -z "${RDIR}" ]
then
   echo "${USAGE}"
   exit 1
fi
echo "Parm 1 -> ${RLEV} : Parm 2 -> ${RDIR}"
#----------------------------------------------
rman nocatalog <<EOF
connect target /
  run {
    allocate channel d1 type disk;
    setlimit channel d1 kbytes 1900000;
    backup incremental level=${RLEV}
      tag db_level_${RLEV}
      format '${RDIR}/rm_l_${RLEV}_%d_%t_%U.bus'
      (database filesperset=25 include current
          controlfile);
    sql "alter system archive log current";
    release channel d1;
```

```
    }
EOF
#----------------------------------------------
#-- Test for success of RMAN operation
if [ $? -ne 0 ]; then
$MAILX -s "RMAN problem with $ORACLE_SID on $BOX" \
$MAIL_LIST <<EOF
Check level ${RLEV} RMAN backups...
EOF
  #
else
  print "RMAN ran okay..."
fi
#----------------------------------------------
exit
```

Assuming this shell file is named *rman_inc.ksh*, invoke it from the O/S command line as follows to take a level 0 backup to be placed in the */ora01/backup* directory:

```
$ rman_inc.ksh 0 /ora01/backup
```

This example checks for usage, runs the necessary RMAN commands to perform an incremental backup, and checks to see whether those commands failed or executed successfully. An appropriate email message is then sent to an individual, or to the list of email addresses in the $MAIL_LIST variable.

Implementing a Catalog

One important decision when using RMAN is deciding whether to use a recovery catalog. This section covers the pros and cons of a catalog and then details catalog implementation issues.

What Is the Catalog?

In many respects, RMAN can be thought of as an Oracle database file backup and restoration utility. RMAN must keep track of many things. When was the last backup taken? Which files were backed up? Which backup sets contain which database files? The answers to these questions can be found in the target control files. Optionally, RMAN can be configured to store this information in a separate database known as the *catalog*.

The catalog consists collectively of a database and a database schema. The schema objects hold the RMAN-specific information for each of your target databases.

Catalog advantages

When you use a catalog repository, you get more flexibility and access to all the features of RMAN. The advantages of using a catalog accrue in the following areas:

- If you are using Oracle8*i*, it can be difficult to recover control files if you don't have a catalog.
- You can retain backup and recovery metadata for long periods of time.
- You can centralize operations.
- RMAN becomes more flexible in certain backup and recovery scenarios.

A catalog enables you to recover your control files in the event that they are all corrupted or lost. If you are not using a catalog, and you haven't backed up your control files via an ALTER DATABASE BACKUP CONTROLFILE command, you could find yourself in the unenviable position of not being able to recover your target.

Another good reason to use a catalog is that information pertaining to your RMAN backup and recovery activities can be stored for very long periods of time. If for any reason you had to use a backup set that was several months old, a catalog provides more flexibility to go back further in time than with the NOCATALOG option.

With a catalog, you can manage all of your backup and recovery activities from one repository. The advantage of this is that if you have multiple databases to maintain, you're storing all of your backup and recovery metadata in one place.

Finally, when using the catalog, you have greater flexibility during certain recovery situations. For example, you can use previous incarnations of the database for recovery.

Catalog disadvantages

While the advantages of the catalog are substantial, there are a few potential headaches that you should be aware of:

- Upgrades and compatibility can be problematic.
- A catalog adds complexity.
- Using a catalog created prior to Oracle Version 8.1.6 with multiple versions of target databases can be problematic.
- A catalog can increase your needs for hardware and DBA resources.

If you're backing up production databases, and you want the most flexibility possible for any given backup and recovery scenario, Oracle recommends that you use a catalog database. However, if you have nonproduction databases for which you want to implement RMAN functionality, but you don't want the overhead of a catalog, you may want to consider just using the target control files.

Using RMAN without a catalog

RMAN can be used out of the box to back up, restore, and recover a database without setting up a catalog. You may decide not to use a catalog because you have limited resources or because you want a quick and easy backup and recovery mechanism for your databases. This section points out the issues you need to be aware of if you choose this route:

- If you are using Oracle8*i* or an earlier version, you may not be able to recover your database if you lose all of your control files. If this happens, you may not be able to recover your database. If you exclusively use the target control files for the repository, you must put into place a mechanism that backs up your control files. (This should be a standard practice anyway.) You should also multiplex your control files to multiple disk drives.

NOTE

If you do not use a catalog, make sure that your control files are backed up via the ALTER DATABASE BACKUP CONTROLFILE command.

- The amount of history maintained about RMAN operations is limited.
- You lose some flexibility returning to previous versions of backup sets. If you discover you have a bad backup set (i.e., it is corrupt or lost), you need to tell RMAN to go to a previous version of a backup. Without a catalog you lose some flexibility when marking backup sets as unusable.
- You may need to increase the size of the *init.ora* parameter CONTROL_FILE_RECORD_KEEP_TIME. This parameter controls the number of days backup and recovery information is stored in the control file before it can be overwritten. The default is seven days. You must ensure that you run your backups at least once during that seven-day period.

Catalog Backup Strategies

If you implement a catalog, it then demands the attention that you would give to any other important production database.

As with any production database, there are various backup and recovery strategies:

- Full export
- Cold backup
- Hot backup
- RMAN backup
- Hot standby
- Recreating catalog

Each method has its advantages and disadvantages that you should weigh based on your business requirements. Some of the significant issues related to each backup method are discussed next.

Full export

A full export is one of the simplest methods to back up a database. The downside to a full export is that you can only recover your database up to the last time you took a full export. If you have to restore your catalog from a full export, ensure that you take full or level 0 backups of all your target databases as soon as possible.

Cold backup

Cold backups are simple to implement but require downtime. If your catalog database is in *archivelog* mode, you can use cold backups to do point-in-time recovery of your catalog if necessary.

Hot backup

Hot backups are slightly more complex to implement than cold backups but have the advantage of keeping the database online during the backup. For these reasons, this is our preferred method for backing up the catalog.

RMAN backup

RMAN can be used to back up your catalog either with another catalog or with the NOCATALOG option. Creating another catalog to back up your catalog adds complexity to your architecture. If you use RMAN with no catalog, make sure that you have a separate mechanism to back up the control files.

Hot standby

Hot standbys let you quickly bring up a standby database if the primary is down. However, hot standbys can be complex to implement and consume more resources.

Recreating a catalog

If you completely lose your catalog and have no usable backups of it, you can recreate it and then reregister and back up your targets. The risk of this method is that during this period, if you lose a target database and its control files you may not be able to recover them.

Catalog Issues

The creation of the catalog database is fairly straightforward. It is, after all, just a database, schema, and objects. Here are some issues you should consider:

- Where to put the database that will host the catalog
- Which database version to use for the catalog
- How to size the catalog
- How to manage multiple target databases

Physical location of the catalog

You should place the catalog database on a different server than the target database. If you fail to do this, you jeopardize

---

backup and recovery operations, because you make it possible to lose both the catalog and target databases.

The catalog can coexist in a database used for other applications. The advantage to this is that you leverage existing resources. The disadvantage is that the performance and availability of your catalog can be affected by other applications within the same database.

Version of catalog

What version of Oracle should you use to create the catalog database? We suggest that the catalog database be created with the latest version of Oracle in your production environment. This helps to minimize compatibility issues and complexity when you start to back up your target databases.

NOTE

Later versions of Oracle8*i* and Oracle9*i* decrease the maintenance issues involved when dealing with multiple versions of target databases.

Sizing the catalog

The size of a catalog database partially depends on how many target databases you need it to support. Here are the space requirements we recommend for a minimal catalog configuration:

- System tablespace: 200 MB
- Temporary tablespace: 20 MB
- Rollback/undo tablespace: 20 MB
- Tablespace for the catalog schema: 20 MB
- Two groups with two members each of online redo logs sized at 2 MB

Depending on the number of targets and the frequency of backups, you will most likely require more space than these minimal settings.

Managing multiple target databases

In an ideal RMAN world, all production databases would be on the same version, and there would be no compatibility or upgrade issues. But as you know, this is rarely the case. It's more likely that you will deal with target databases that span Oracle versions from 8.0.4 to 9.0.x. If that's the case, you have some choices to make.

Each choice has a positive or negative impact on the level of compatibility and on the maintenance issues that are likely to appear. The trick, of course, is to make the appropriate choice for your organization, and in doing so, limit the downside effects. The nature of your choices is driven by three independent variables:

- The version of the target database
- The version of the catalog database
- The version of the objects created within the catalog schema

With this said, your options for creating a catalog to handle multiple targets implemented using multiple versions can be boiled down to the following:

- Use a version-specific catalog database and a catalog schema based on that version for each target database.
- Use one catalog database with version-specific catalog schemas for the different targets.
- Use one catalog database for all your target databases, created with the highest version of Oracle available, and a catalog schema created with the corresponding highest version of the *rman* binary.

Creating a Catalog

The examples in this section provide details for creating a catalog database and registering a target database within the catalog. These examples assume that your catalog database is on a different host than your target database. They are implemented with Oracle9*i*, but the steps are the same for Oracle8*i*.

To create a recovery catalog, follow these steps:

1. Create a specific tablespace to hold the catalog objects.
2. Create a catalog schema.
3. Issue appropriate grants.
4. Create the schema objects.

In the following examples, we use the label "901" simply to indicate the version of the catalog database, in this case Oracle Version 9.0.1.

The first step, tablespace creation, is straightforward:

```
SQL> CREATE TABLESPACE rman_901_cat
     DATAFILE '/d01/oradata/brdstn/rman_901_cat_01.dbf'
       SIZE 50M;
```

Now that you have a tablespace to store your schema objects, you can create the schema:

```
SQL> CREATE USER rman_901
     IDENTIFIED BY rman_901_pwd
     DEFAULT TABLESPACE rman_901_cat
     TEMPORARY TABLESPACE temp
     QUOTA UNLIMITED ON rman_901_cat;
```

Before you can create the catalog objects, you need to grant special privileges to your new schema. These privileges, granted through the RECOVERY_CATALOG_OWNER role, lets the schema manage its catalog objects.

```
SQL> GRANT recovery_catalog_owner TO rman_901;
```

You can view the privileges that this role grants by looking in *dba_sys_privs*:

```
SQL> SELECT PRIVILEGE FROM dba_sys_privs
     WHERE GRANTEE = 'RECOVERY_CATALOG_OWNER';

PRIVILEGE
-----------------------------------------
ALTER SESSION
CREATE CLUSTER
CREATE DATABASE LINK
CREATE PROCEDURE
CREATE SEQUENCE
CREATE SESSION
CREATE SYNONYM
CREATE TABLE
CREATE TRIGGER
CREATE VIEW

10 rows selected.
```

You can now create the catalog objects within your new schema. In order to perform this step, invoke RMAN, connect to your newly created catalog schema, and issue the *create catalog* command. If you don't specify a tablespace with the *create catalog* command, the catalog objects are created in the default tablespace assigned to the catalog owner.

```
$ rman catalog rman_901/rman_901_pwd

Recovery Manager: Release 9.0.1.0.0 - Production

connected to recovery catalog database
recovery catalog is not installed

RMAN> create catalog;

recovery catalog created

RMAN> exit
```

At this point, you now have an operational RMAN catalog.

Registering a Target Database

After creating a catalog, the next logical step is to register a target database. You won't be able to back up the target with the catalog unless the target is registered. On the box that hosts the target database, invoke RMAN, connect to both the target and the catalog, and issue the *register database* command. In this example we are registering a target database identified as BRDSTN:

```
$ rman target / catalog rman_901/rman_901@rman_catalog

Recovery Manager: Release 9.0.1.0.0 - Production

connected to target database: BRDSTN (DBID=664610428)
connected to recovery catalog

RMAN> register database;

database registered in recovery catalog
starting full resync of recovery catalog
full resync complete
```

The catalog is now ready to store information about target database backup activities. You can view information in the catalog via various RMAN commands such as *report schema*; see the "RMAN Command Reference" section for details.

Stored Catalog Scripts

Storing scripts in the catalog is another common technique saves RMAN commands for reuse. To use this method you must have a catalog database.

Storing a Script

To store a script you need to connect to both the catalog and the target. You need to connect to the catalog so that RMAN knows where to store the scripts, and you need to connect to the target so that RMAN knows which target database the stored script is associated with.

Once a connection to the target and catalog is established, you can store a script using either the *create script* or *replace script* commands. The *replace script* command creates a new script or replaces a previously stored script by the name under which you store the script. The following example creates a script to do a full backup of a database:

```
$ rman target / catalog rman_901/rman_901_pwd@rman_catalog

Recovery Manager: Release 9.0.1.0.0 - Production

connected to target database: BRDSTN (DBID=664610428)
connected to recovery catalog database
RMAN> replace script full_back{
2> allocate channel d1 type disk;
3> backup full format
4> '/d0102/backup/rman_%d_%U.bus' database;
5> }

replaced script full_back
```

This stores the script, which is named *full_back*, in the catalog. This does not execute the script. To run the commands that you've just stored, you need to execute the script.

Executing a Stored Script

After you've stored your scripts, you will want to run them. Once connections have been established to both the catalog and target database, you can call the stored script via the *execute script* command:

```
$ rman target / catalog rman_901/rman_901_pwd@rman_catalog

Recovery Manager: Release 9.0.1.0.0 - Production

connected to target database: BRDSTN (DBID=664610428)
connected to recovery catalog database

RMAN> run {execute script full_back;}

executing script: full_back
```

You can also call stored scripts from other stored scripts. This allows you to modularize your RMAN commands. For example, you may want one script to allocate a channel, another to release a channel, and a third to run a *backup* command. For example, create a file called *stsc.sto* and place within it the following commands:

```
# This script allocates a channel.
replace script alloc_disk {
  allocate channel d1 type disk;
}

# This script releases the channel.
replace script rel_disk {
  release channel d1;
}

# This script does a full backup.
replace script run_backup{
  execute script alloc_disk;
  backup full format '/d0102/backup/rman_%d_%U.bus'
    database;
  execute script rel_disk;
}
```

Then, to execute the file and store all of the scripts, issue the following command from the O/S prompt:

```
$ rman target / catalog rman_901/rman_901_pwd@rman_catalog
  @stsc.sto log=str.log
```

The scripts will be stored in the catalog. And if you look at the log file, *str.log*, you will see the informational messages. Three scripts are stored, with *run_backup* being the main script. That script, in turn, invokes the other two scripts as part of a full backup operation. The following example shows how to initiate this operation from RMAN:

```
$ rman target / catalog rman_901/rman_901_pwd@rman_catalog

Recovery Manager: Release 9.0.1.0.0 - Production

RMAN> run {execute script run_backup;}
```

The *run_backup* script allocates a channel by invoking the *alloc_disk* script, takes a full backup using the *backup* command, and then releases the channel with a call to the *rel_disk* script.

Viewing a Stored Script

To view the stored catalog scripts from within RMAN, there's a *print script* command:

```
print script script_name;
```

To view the script that we just stored, invoke RMAN, connect to both the target and the catalog, and then print the script:

```
$ rman target / catalog rman_901/rman_901_pwd@rman_catalog
RMAN> print script full_back;
```

If you want to see all source code stored in the catalog, you can do so by querying from two RMAN views: rc_stored_script and rc_stored_script_line:

```
SQL> desc rc_stored_script
 Name                            Null?    Type
 ------------------------------- -------- ----------
 DB_KEY                          NOT NULL NUMBER
 DB_NAME                         NOT NULL VARCHAR2(8)
 SCRIPT_NAME                     NOT NULL VARCHAR2(100)

SQL> desc rc_stored_script_line
 Name                            Null?    Type
 ------------------------------- -------- ----------
 DB_KEY                          NOT NULL NUMBER
 SCRIPT_NAME                     NOT NULL VARCHAR2(100)
 LINE                            NOT NULL NUMBER
 TEXT                            NOT NULL VARCHAR2(1024)
```

To view all stored script code associated with your target database, log in with SQL*Plus as the schema that owns the objects in the catalog and run the following script:

```
COLUMN script_name FORMAT A10
COLUMN text        FORMAT A65
```

```
SELECT
  a.script_name,
  a.text
FROM rc_stored_script_line a,
     rc_stored_script       b
WHERE a.db_key = b.db_key
AND   b.db_name='YOUR_TARGET_DATABASE_NAME'
ORDER BY
  a.line
/
```

Run the script from SQL*Plus, and the output will look something like:

```
SCRIPT_NAM TEXT
---------- -----------------------------------
full_back  {
full_back     allocate channel d1 type disk;
full_back     backup full format
   '/d0102/backup/rman_%d_%U.bus'
full_back     database;
full_back  }
```

Deleting a Stored Script

To delete a stored script from the catalog, use the command:

```
RMAN> delete script script_name;
```

in which *script_name* is the name of the script you want to delete.

Backups

This section provides a series of RMAN and *korn* shell scripts that illustrate backing up a database and its separate components. RMAN can back up datafiles, control files, archived redo files, and backup pieces. RMAN does not back up the online redo logs.

For a database to be backed up it must be in *mount* mode or open. The database needs to at least be in *mount* mode, because RMAN needs to access the target database control file before performing a backup.

Full Database Offline Backup

For offline backups, the database needs to be shut down and restarted in *mount* mode. The database does not have to be in *archivelog* mode.

Here's a shell script for an Oracle9*i* database that shuts down the database, mounts it, backs it up, and opens it:

```
#!/bin/ksh

rman target / <<EOF
shutdown immediate;
startup mount;
backup database format
  '/d99/rmanback/brdstn/rman_%d_%t_%U.bus';
alter database open;
EOF
exit
```

The following shell script takes a full backup of an Oracle8*i* database. Notice that the command syntax is a little more verbose than that needed for Oracle9*i*. For Oracle8*i*, the syntax requires you to place the *allocate* and *backup* commands within the *run{}* command.

```
#!/bin/ksh

rman target / nocatalog <<EOF
shutdown immediate;
```

```
startup mount;
run {
allocate channel d1 type disk;
backup database format
  '/d99/rmanback/brdstn/rman_%d_%t_%U.bus';
}
alter database open;
EOF
Exit
```

<hr>

NOTE

We've used the *format* parameter in both examples to
provide a specific location and unique name for the backup pieces. If the *format* parameter is not used, the backup pieces will be directed to *$ORACLE_HOME/dbs*.
Please refer to Table 1-1 in the "RMAN Command Reference" section.

<hr>

Full Database Online Backup

For online backups, the database is open for use and must be
in *archivelog* mode. If you're using Oracle9*i*, the syntax can
be fairly simple:

```
RMAN> backup database format
2> '/d99/rmanback/brdstn/rman_%d_%t_%U.bus';
```

<hr>

NOTE

Unlike traditional online (hot) backups, RMAN does not
put tablespaces in backup mode. No extra redo is generated. For high-transaction databases, this can lead to significant resource savings.

<hr>

Again, note that with Oracle8*i*, the syntax is a bit different
with respect to the *run{}* command:

```
RMAN> run {
2> allocate channel d1 type disk;
3> backup database format
```

```
4> '/d99/rmanback/brdstn/rman_%d_%t_%U.bus';
5> }
```

Backing Up a Tablespace

The ability to specify only a subset of tablespaces in a backup
operation can add flexibility to your backup strategy. For
Oracle9i, the syntax can be fairly simple:

```
RMAN> backup tablespace system, users format
2> '/d99/rmanback/brdstn/rman_bckup_%d_%t_%U.bus';
```

Once again, note that with Oracle8i, the syntax is a bit different with respect to the *run{}* command:

```
RMAN> run {
2> allocate channel d1 type disk;
3> backup format
4> '/d99/rmanback/brdstn/rman_bckup_%d_%t_%U.bus'
5> tablespace system, users include current controlfile;
6> }
```

Backing Up a Datafile

With datafiles, you can either back them up by number or by
name. With Oracle9i, the syntax is straightforward. If you're
performing a disk-based backup and know the numbers of
the datafiles that you want to back up, the command is:

```
RMAN> backup datafile 1,2;
```

For an Oracle8i disk-based backup, the syntax is:

```
RMAN> run {
2> allocate channel d1 type disk;
3> backup format
4> '/d99/rmanback/brdstn/rman_bckup_%d_%t_%U.bus'
5> datafile 1, 2;
6> }
```

Alternatively, you can tell RMAN the name of a specific datafile that you want to back up:

```
RMAN> run {
2> allocate channel d1 type disk;
```

```
3> backup format
4> '/d99/rmanback/brdstn/rman_bckup_%d_%t_%U.bus'
5> '/d01/oradata/workprd/users_01.dbf';
6> }
```

To specify more than one datafile by name, list the names separated by commas.

Backing Up Control Files

A nice feature of Oracle9*i* is its ability to configure the control file to be backed up automatically whenever you issue a *backup* or *copy* command. You can do this by using the *configure* command as follows:

```
RMAN> configure controlfile autobackup on;
```

Or, if you want to manually back up an Oracle9*i* control file:

```
RMAN> backup current controlfile;
```

Here's an example that backs up the control file via a shell script that works both for Oracle9*i* and Oracle8*i*:

```
#!/bin/ksh
# File: backup_ctrl.ksh
#------------------------------------------------
export ORACLE_HOME=/d00/app/oracle/product/9.0.0
export ORACLE_SID=brdstn
export PATH=/usr/sbin:/usr/bin:$ORACLE_HOME/bin
export MAILX="/usr/ucb/Mail"
export MAIL_LIST="chaya@garam.com"
#------------------------------------------------
BOX=`uname -a | awk '{print$2}'`
#------------------------------------------------
date
#------------------------------------------------
rman nocatalog log=rman_control.log <<EOF
  connect target /
  run {
    allocate channel d1 type disk;
    setlimit channel d1 kbytes 1900000;
    backup
      format '/d99/rmanback/brdstn/rman_cntl_%d_%t_%U.bct'
      (current controlfile);
    release channel d1;
```

```
    }
EOF
#
if [ $? -ne 0 ]; then
$MAILX -s "RMAN problem with $ORACLE_SID on $BOX" \
$MAIL_LIST <<EOF
Check control file RMAN backups...
EOF
    #
else
    print "RMAN controlfile backup ran okay..."
fi
#-----------------------------------------------
date
#-----------------------------------------------
```

Backing Up Archived Redo Log Files

With Oracle9i, the syntax for backing up archived redo log
files is fairly simple:

```
RMAN> backup archivelog all;
```

Another Oracle9i technique is to use the *backup* command's
plus archivelog clause to include the archive redo log files as
part of a backup. This creates at least two backup pieces, one
for the datafiles, and one for the archived redo log files:

```
RMAN> backup database format
2> '/d00/backup/rman_%U.bus' plus archivelog;
```

Here's a simple script that works with both Oracle8i and
Oracle9i to back up all the archived redo log files for a target:

```
RMAN> run {
2> allocate channel t1 type 'sbt_tape';
3> backup filesperset 5 format
4> '/d0100/backup/ar_%d_%t.bus' (archivelog all );
5> }
```

NOTE

One nice feature of RMAN is that it knows when an archived redo file has been completely written to disk. Therefore, RMAN will not attempt to back up any partially written archived redo log files.

Here's another example that uses a shell script to execute the RMAN commands to back up the archived redo log files. When executed, all archived redo log files generated within a three-day period will be included in the backup set.

```ksh
#!/bin/ksh
# File: backup_arch.ksh
#----------------------------------------------
export ORACLE_HOME=/d00/app/oracle/product/9.0.0
export ORACLE_SID=brdstn
export PATH=/usr/sbin:/usr/bin:$ORACLE_HOME/bin
export MAILX="/usr/ucb/Mail"
export MAIL_LIST="heeraa@chamak.com"
#----------------------------------------------
BOX=`uname -a | awk '{print$2}'`
#----------------------------------------------
date
#----------------------------------------------
rman nocatalog log=rman_arch_back.log <<EOF
  connect target sys/pwd
  run {
    allocate channel d1 type disk;
    setlimit channel d1 kbytes 1900000;
    backup
      format '/d99/backup/brdstn/arch_%d_%t.bus'
      filesperset=50
      archivelog from time 'sysdate-3';
    release channel d1;
  }
EOF
#
if [ $? -ne 0 ]; then
$MAILX -s "RMAN problem with $ORACLE_SID on $BOX" \
$MAIL_LIST <<EOF
```

```
Check archived redo RMAN backups...
EOF
  #
else
  print "RMAN archive backups ran okay..."
fi
#------------------------------------------------
date
#------------------------------------------------
```

NOTE

If you have a non-RMAN process remove the redo log files, the control files or the optional recovery catalog will not be aware that they are no longer accessible. Consequently, you would have to periodically issue the command:

```
RMAN> change archivelog all validate;
```

Therefore, you should allow RMAN to remove them from the filesystem when they are no longer necessary.

Incremental Backups

One of the most impressive features of RMAN is its ability to perform incremental backups. Recall that with traditional file-based backups—such as hot or cold—all blocks in a database datafile are copied, whether they have been used or not. RMAN has the ability to detect which blocks in a datafile have changed since the last backup and will copy only those modified blocks.

NOTE

When RMAN copies only the modified blocks during a backup, this is called *compression*. If there are unused or unmodified blocks in a datafile, RMAN will skip those blocks.

Skipping unmodified blocks gives RMAN a big advantage over file-based backups in that the resources required to do a backup or restore can be considerably less. Additionally, this means that the backup time and tape/disk space required correlates to the number of changes made to the database, and not necessarily to the size of the database. For very large databases, this alone can necessitate the use of RMAN.

Much of the nomenclature around incremental backups contains the term *level*. The basic idea behind RMAN level-based backups is to back up only blocks that have been modified since the previous backup. Incremental backups can be applied to the database, tablespaces, or datafiles. Oracle refers to this usage of levels as a *multilevel incremental backup*. These levels can range from level 0 to a maximum of level 4.

There are two flavors of incremental backups—differential and cumulative. A *differential* incremental backup tells RMAN to back up blocks that have changed since level n or lower. For example, if you take a level 1 differential backup, you will back up blocks that have changed since the previous level 1 backup. Differential backups are the default incremental backup mode.

NOTE

If you take an incremental backup higher than level 0, and no prior level 0 exists, RMAN automatically creates a level 0 backup.

A cumulative incremental backup instructs RMAN to back up blocks that have changed since level $n-1$ or lower. For example, if you take a level 1 cumulative backup, RMAN will back up blocks that have changed since the most recent level 0 backup.

> **NOTE**
>
> A full backup backs up the exact same blocks as a level 0.
> The difference between a full backup and a level 0 back-
> up is that a full backup is not known to any subsequent
> incremental backups. Therefore, they cannot be used as a
> basis when applying incremental backups during a recov-
> ery operation. A full backup is the default backup type if
> no incremental level is specified.

Why all the choices? A differential backup takes less space
and time to perform but requires more time to restore. It follows that a cumulative backup takes more space and time to
perform but less time to restore. So it becomes a tradeoff
issue; do you want to minimize your backup time or minimize your restore time? We prefer to minimize our restore
time, and therefore, we use cumulative backups. For small
databases, we recommend daily RMAN level 0 backups.

Here's an Oracle9*i* cumulative backup example in which you
tell RMAN to back up all blocks that have been modified
since the most recent level 3 or lower backup and to skip
read-only tablespaces:

```
RMAN> backup incremental level 4 cumulative database
2> skip readonly;
```

Here's an Oracle8*i* differential backup example that backs up
all blocks that have changed since the most recent level 1 or
lower backup:

```
RMAN> run {allocate channel d1 type disk;
2> backup incremental level 1 format
3> '/d0101/backup/rman_%U.bus' database;}
```

Backup Tips

Now that we've covered multiple backup scenarios, let's look
at various commands designed to report on the integrity of
backups or enhance the performance of backup operations.

Validating backups

One nice feature of RMAN is the ability to report on the status of backups. The simplest way to view backup information is via the *list backup* command.

```
RMAN> list backup;
```

The output of *list backup* displays information such as the name, level, completion time, and status of each backup. Additionally, RMAN also has a nice way to verify whether the backup files are restorable. You accomplish this by issuing the *restore database validate* command. This command doesn't actually restore any datafiles, it just validates that the contents of the backup sets can be restored if necessary. The following example works with both Oracle8*i* and Oracle9*i*:

```
RMAN> run {
2> allocate channel d1 type disk;
3> restore database validate;
4> }
```

Configuring channels

A handy feature that comes with Oracle9*i* is the ability to alter the default channel characteristics. Once altered, these characteristics are stored in the control file, and persist from RMAN session to RMAN session. The following example changes the default disk rate and format style:

```
RMAN> configure channel device type disk
2> rate 1000000 format '/d99/rmanback/rman_%U.bus';
```

To see all of your configuration settings, use the *show all* command:

```
RMAN> show all;

RMAN configuration parameters are:
CONFIGURE RETENTION POLICY TO REDUNDANCY 1; # default
CONFIGURE BACKUP OPTIMIZATION OFF; # default
CONFIGURE DEFAULT DEVICE TYPE TO DISK; # default
CONFIGURE CONTROLFILE AUTOBACKUP OFF; # default
CONFIGURE CONTROLFILE AUTOBACKUP FORMAT FOR DEVICE TYPE
  DISK TO '%F'; # default
```

```
CONFIGURE DEVICE TYPE DISK PARALLELISM 1; # default
CONFIGURE DATAFILE BACKUP COPIES FOR DEVICE TYPE DISK TO
  1; # default
CONFIGURE ARCHIVELOG BACKUP COPIES FOR DEVICE TYPE DISK TO
  1; # default
CONFIGURE CHANNEL DEVICE TYPE DISK RATE 1000000 FORMAT
  '/d99/rmanback/rman_%U.bus';
CONFIGURE MAXSETSIZE TO UNLIMITED; # default
CONFIGURE SNAPSHOT CONTROLFILE NAME TO '/d00/app/oracle
  product/9.0.0/dbs/snapcf_dev900.f'; # default
```

In the output of a *show all* command, if a default setting has
not been altered, it is followed by the text # default.

To clear the channel characteristics, use the *configure clear*
command. The following example sets the device type back
to your disk's default:

```
RMAN> configure default device type clear;
```

Parallelism of backups

In order to improve performance, RMAN can break out certain commands and use multiple, parallel processes to execute the issued command. This does not mean that if you
issue five RMAN commands, RMAN will try to parallelize
and run those five commands at the same time, but rather
that each individual command will be parallelized.

A good example of parallelization is using a *backup* command. If you allocate multiple channels, RMAN simultaneously uses multiple processes to work on the command,
writing data simultaneously through all channels:

```
RMAN> configure device type disk parallelism 3;
RMAN> backup database format '/d99/rmanback/rman_%U.bus';
```

In effect, this uses three concurrent processes to back up the
database.

Tagging a backup

Sometimes it's nice to name a backup set based on your
nomenclature. For example, you may want to distinguish

between daily or weekly backups, or you may want to distinguish easily between various incremental-level backups. One way to do this is to tag your backup set with a name of your choosing. You do this via the *tag* keyword in the *backup* command. For example, the following example tags a level 3 backup with the name *inc_level_3*:

```
RMAN> backup incremental level 3 tag inc_level_3 format
2> '/d99/rmanback/rman_%U.bus';
```

Tags can be used with the *list* command to locate backup sets quickly and can also be used with the *restore* and *switch* commands. The same tag name can be used across multiple backup sets; in other words, it doesn't have to be unique. When a tag name that you reference is not unique, RMAN uses the most recent backup set with the given tag name.

As an example, the following *list* command reports on the previous backup we tagged as *inc_level_3*:

```
RMAN> list backuppiece tag=inc_level_3;
```

Restoring Files

In general there are three steps involved in restoring files:

1. Ensure that the target database is started in the appropriate mode for the restoration operation. For lost control files, this will be *nomount* mode. If the entire database needs to be restored, this will be *mount* mode. If datafiles that don't belong to the SYSTEM tablespace are damaged, you have the option of keeping the database open and taking only the tablespace(s)/datafile(s) that needs to be restored offline.

2. Start RMAN and connect to the target and recovery catalog if one is being used.

3. Run the appropriate RMAN RESTORE command to bring back required files. The requested files and the appropriate archived redo log files will be restored.

Once the necessary files are restored, you need to recover your database and open it for use. You can recover the database from either RMAN, SQL*Plus, or Server Manager (Oracle8i only).

Restoring and Recovering All Datafiles

In this scenario, it is assumed that your control files are still accessible. Your first step is to make sure that the target database is shut down:

```
SQL> connect sys/harakhat as SYSDBA;
SQL> shutdown abort;
ORACLE instance shut down.
```

Next, you need to start up your target database in *mount* mode. RMAN cannot restore datafiles unless the database is at least in *mount* mode, because RMAN needs to be able to access the control file to determine which backup sets are necessary to recover the database. If the control file isn't available, you have to recover it first. Issue the STARTUP MOUNT command shown in the following example to mount the database:

```
SQL> startup mount;
Oracle instance started.

Total System Global Area   309809312 bytes
Fixed Size                 7388 bytes
Variable Size              145715200 bytes
Redo Buffers               180224 bytes
Database mounted.
```

Since backup set files are created in an RMAN-specific format, you must use RMAN to restore the datafiles. To use RMAN, connect to the target database:

```
$ rman target / catalog rman_901/rman_901_pwd@rman_catalog
Recovery Manager Release 9.0.1.0.0 - Production
connected to target database: BRDSTN (DBID=664610428)
connected to recovery catalog
```

The remainder of this example shows how to restore all of the datafiles of the target database. RMAN will go to its last good backup set and restore the datafiles to the state they were in when that backup set was created.

When restoring database files with Oracle9i, RMAN reads the datafile header and makes the determination as to whether the file needs to be restored. The recovery is done by allocating a channel for I/O and then issuing the RMAN *restore database* command.

With Oracle9i, you don't need to allocate a channel explicitly. Instead, you can use the *default channel* mode:

```
RMAN> restore database;
RMAN> recover database;
RMAN> alter database open;
```

For Oracle8i, the ALLOCATE, RESTORE, and RECOVER commands need to be enclosed by the *run{}* command:

```
RMAN> run {
2> allocate channel d1 type disk;
3> restore database;
4> recover database;
5> alter database open; }
```

Or alternatively, once RMAN has restored the datafiles, you can use SQL*Plus to recover the database and open it for use:

```
$ sqlplus /nolog
SQL> connect sys/hinghoda as SYSDBA;
SQL> recover database;
SQL> alter database open;
```

Restoring Specific Tablespaces/Datafiles

With Oracle9i, restoring a tablespace or a datafile can be a very straightforward task. If you are recovering the tablespace or datafile while the database is up, you must first take the tablespace or datafile offline. In the following example, we restore and recover the USERS tablespace:

```
RMAN> restore tablespace users;
RMAN> recover tablespace users;
```

Instead of a tablespace, you can restore and recover a specific datafile:

```
RMAN> restore datafile
2> '/d0101/oradata/brdstn/users_01.dbf'
RMAN> recover datafile
2> '/d0101/oradata/brdstn/users_01.dbf'
```

With Oracle8i, the syntax for restoring a tablespace is only slightly more involved, because the ALLOCATE, RESTORE, and RECOVER commands are used, and they must be wrapped by the *run{}* command:

```
RMAN> run {
2> allocate channel d1 type disk;
3> restore tablespace users;
4> recover tablespace users; }
```

Restoring Read-Only Tablespaces

Once you back up a read-only tablespace, you don't need to back it up again. However, you may want to periodically back up your read-only tablespaces so that in the event of a recovery, RMAN doesn't have to retrieve a backup set that may be on tape and offsite. RMAN does not require any archived redo log files to restore and recover a read-only tablespace. Also, to recover a read-only tablespace you do not need to bring down the database. The steps are:

1. Take the tablespace offline.
2. Restore the tablespace or the appropriate datafiles.
3. Bring the tablespace online. No recovery is necessary.

For example:

```
RMAN> sql 'alter tablespace old_rnd offline';

RMAN> restore tablespace old_rnd;

RMAN> sql 'alter tablespace old_rnd online';
```

Point-in-Time Recovery

If your database is in *archivelog* mode, you can do point-in-time recovery. This type of recovery is performed against the entire database and not against a single datafile or tablespace. It should not be confused with tablespace point-in-time recovery (RMAN TSPITR). The following Oracle9*i* example uses RMAN to restore the datafiles and then uses SQL*Plus to perform a cancel-based recovery:

```
RMAN> restore database;
```

```
SQL> recover database until cancel;
```

Once you have recovered your database to the appropriate point, you can open it for use. Since you are doing a point-in-time recovery, you need to open the database with the *resetlogs* parameter:

```
SQL> alter database open resetlogs;
```

Since the logs were reset, it is crucial that an immediate backup be taken of the database. Additionally, if a recovery catalog is being used, a new incarnation of the database has been created and must be made known to the catalog via the *reset database* command.

Restoring Control Files

In an ideal world you'll never use RMAN to restore a control file. But if something catastrophic happens, and you lose all control files, here are the steps for getting them back:

1. Start up your database in *nomount* mode.
2. Run the RMAN RESTORE CONTROLFILE command.

NOTE

With Oracle9*i*, if you are not using a catalog, you can still restore the control file if you have used RMAN's autobackup feature to back it up with each backup that you do.

The following examples assume that you are using a catalog. First, here's the simplest Oracle9*i* syntax for restoring a control file:

```
RMAN> startup nomount;
RMAN> restore controlfile;
```

For Oracle8*i*, you need to use the *run{}* command syntax:

```
RMAN> run {
2> allocate channel t1 type sbt_tape;
3> restore controlfile;}
```

Restoring Archived Redo Log Files

When you issue a RECOVER command from RMAN, the RMAN utility first looks on disk to see if the necessary archived redo log files are present. If they aren't, RMAN retrieves them from any RMAN archived redo log file backups that you've taken. If you want to explicitly tell RMAN to bring back your archived redo log files, you use the RESTORE ARCHIVELOG command.

NOTE

For datafile recovery, if there is an incremental backup available, RMAN uses an incremental backup over an archived redo log file.

The following Oracle9*i* example sets a location where the archived redo log files are written and then restores them. Even in Oracle9*i*, this command must be executed from within the *run{}* command.

```
RMAN> run {
2> set archivelog destination to '/d00/backup/';
3> restore archivelog all; }
```

If the archived redo log files aren't on disk, or if they haven't been backed up, you could be in trouble. Here's an Oracle9*i* example showing how to restore a tablespace and then use the RECOVER command to automatically rebuild and apply

---

the archived redo log files that are not on disk but have been backed up via RMAN:

```
RMAN> restore tablespace users;
RMAN> recover tablespace users;
```

RMAN Command Reference

It is beyond the scope of this book to detail the ins and outs of every RMAN command. There's simply not enough room. We do provide the syntax for every command. We have also provided the syntax for Oracle8i and Oracle9i. And we provide examples for the most frequently used commands.

Common Keywords

Many keywords are used in many different commands throughout this syntax section. To save space, we list these common keywords first.

allocOperand
> See "allocOperand" later in the "Command-Line Syntax" section.

DBID
> A unique number that identifies a database.

BACKUPSET
> Specifies the backup set to be used for an operation.

CHANNEL channel_id
> Specifies a communication channel that RMAN uses to communicate with an I/O device.

CHECK LOGICAL
> Tests blocks for logical corruption, which is then logged in the alert log and trace files. Additionally, the ranges of corrupt blocks can be queried in V\$BACKUP_CORRUPTION. Ranges of corrupt blocks can be recovered with the Oracle9i BLOCK RECOVER command.

DATAFILE
Specifies a datafile by name or by number.

DATAFILECOPY
Indicates that image copies of datafiles should be used.

DEVICE TYPE deviceSpecifier
Indicates the type of device that should be used for an operation.

FORMAT 'format_string'
Specifies the name and location for backup pieces. Various masks, described in Table 1-1, can be used as part of the format string.

LEVEL integer
Indicates the backup level to perform.

TABLESPACE tablespace_name
Specifies a tablespace name.

TAG tag_name
Specifies an arbitrary tag name for backups, file copies, archived logs, and control file copies.

UNTIL untilClause
Used by various RMAN commands to specify an upper limit for time, System Change Number (SCN), or log sequence numbers.

Table 1-1. Format string masks

Mask	Description
%c	Copy number of the backup piece
%d	Database name
%D	Day of the month (DD)
%M	Month of the year (MM)
%F	A unique name based on the DBID (a unique number that identifies a database), day of month, month, year, and a sequence number
%n	The database name, right-padded to a maximum length of eight characters

Table 1-1. Format string masks (continued)

Mask	Description
%u	An eight-character name representing the backup set and the time it was created
%p	Piece number of each file within the backup set; the number starts at 1 and increments by one for each file that is created
%U	A unique filename generated by combining %u_%p_%c
%s	Backup set number
%t	Timestamp of the backup set
%T	Year, month, and day in YYYYMMDD format

Common Clauses

Just as there are many common keywords used by many commands, there are also common clauses. Clauses in syntax diagrams can be identified by the pattern of their name, in which the second and subsequent words are initial-capped. For example: connectStringSpec, backupOperand, and backupSpecOperand are all clauses. If a clause is not defined following the command in which it appears, it is a *common clause*. Common clauses are defined alphabetically amongst the commands.

Command-Line Syntax

You can invoke RMAN using a number of command-line options. These are shown in the following syntax diagrams.

Oracle9i syntax

```
RMAN [parameter [parameter...]]

parameter :=
{ TARGET [=] connectStringSpec
| { CATALOG [=] connectStringSpec | NOCATALOG }
| AUXILIARY [=] connectStringSpec
| LOG [=] [']filename[']
| APPEND
| { CMDFILE [=] | @ } [']filename[']
```

```
  | MSGNO
  | TRACE [=] [']filename[']
  | DEBUG [[=] { ALL | debugType [,debugType ...] }
  [LEVEL [=] integer]]
  | SEND [=] 'command'
  | PIPE [=] [']pipe_name[']
  | TIMEOUT [=] integer
  }
```

Oracle8i syntax

```
  RMAN [parameter [parameter...]]

  parameter :=
  { TARGET [=] connectStringSpec
  | { CATALOG [=] connectStringSpec | NOCATALOG }
  | AUXILIARY [=] connectStringSpec
  | LOG [=] [']filename[']
  | APPEND
  | { CMDFILE [=] | @ } [']filename[']
  | MSGNO
  | TRACE [=] [']filename[']
  | DEBUG
  | SEND [=] 'command'
  }
```

Keywords

TARGET

Specifies the target database.

CATALOG

Specifies the optional recovery catalog database.

AUXILIARY

Specifies the optional auxiliary database.

LOG filename

Specifies a filename for command output. If the file already exists, it will be overwritten unless you use APPEND.

APPEND
> Appends command output to the log file. Creates the log file if it does not already exist. The log file will be over-written if you don't use this keyword.

MSGNO
> Displays RMAN message numbers.

TRACE
> Traces and logs RMAN commands to an output file.

DEBUG
> Displays verbose SQL execution messages.

PIPE
> Allows for RMAN commands to be issued via the DBMS_PIPE package. Pipes may also be used for output purposes.

TIMEOUT
> Used in conjunction with the PIPE command; it causes an RMAN session to terminate within a specified time limit.

SEND
> Sends vendor specified commands to all channels when using a media management layer.

@

Runs RMAN commands stored in an O/S file. If the path is not specified, the file is assumed to exist in the directory from which the RMAN session was initiated.

Syntax

> *@filename*

Example

```
RMAN> @full_back.rmn
```

@@

Runs RMAN commands stored in an O/S file. The double-at sign (@@) has a special meaning when the command is executed from within a script file. It indicates to RMAN that the file to execute is located in the same directory as the parent script.

Syntax

```
@@filename
```

Example

In this example we have two scripts. The first, *backup_full*, contains the second, @@*backup_tablespaces*:

```
RMAN> @backup_full
```

When *backup_full* calls *backup_tablespaces*, RMAN will look for the *backup_tablespaces* script in *backup_full*'s directory.

ALLOCATE CHANNEL

Creates a communication channel for the purpose of performing input/output. Must be executed from within the RUN command.

NOTE

Many of the Oracle8*i* ALLOCATE CHANNEL commands, such as KBYTES and READRATE, have been deprecated. Refer to the CONFIGURE command for the preferred syntax.

Oracle9i syntax

```
ALLOCATE [AUXILIARY] CHANNEL [']channel_id[']
{ DEVICE TYPE [=] deviceSpecifier | NAME [=] 'channel_
  name' }
[allocOperand [allocOperand ...]];
```

Oracle8i syntax

```
ALLOCATE [AUXILIARY] CHANNEL [']channel_id[']
{ TYPE [=] deviceSpecifier | NAME [=] deviceSpecifier }
[allocOperand [allocOperand ...]];
```

Keywords

NAME 'channel_name'
    The name of the I/O device

Examples

In the following example, one channel of type disk is established.
A backup is then performed. The backup pieces are directed to
the default location: *$ORACLE_HOME/dbs*.

```
RMAN> run {
2> allocate channel d1 type disk;
3> backup database;
4> }
```

In this next example, the backup pieces are created within the
directory specified by the FORMAT subclause. A mask of %U
provides each backup piece with a unique name.

```
RMAN> run {
2> allocate channel d1 type disk format
3> '/d99/backups/r_%U';
4> backup database; }
```

ALLOCATE CHANNEL FOR MAINTENANCE

Conducts maintenance on channels, and when doing so is used in
conjunction with the CHANGE or CROSSCHECK commands.

Oracle9i syntax

```
ALLOCATE CHANNEL FOR MAINTENANCE
  DEVICE TYPE [=] deviceSpecifier
  [allocOperand [allocOperand ...]];
```

Oracle8i syntax

```
ALLOCATE CHANNEL FOR
    { MAINTENANCE | DELETE }
    { TYPE [=] deviceSpecifier
    | NAME [=]'channel_name' }
    [ allocOperand [allocOperand ...]];
```

Example

In this example, a channel is allocated to delete a backup piece:

```
RMAN> allocate channel for maintenance type disk;
RMAN> change backuppiece '/d99/backups/1ccn3ed4_1_1'
2> delete;
RMAN> release channel;
```

allocOperand

A clause allowing the characteristics of a channel to be changed.

Oracle9i syntax

```
allocOperand :=
{ PARMS [=] 'channel_parms'
| CONNECT [=] connectStringSpec
| DEBUG [=] integer
| FORMAT [=] 'format_string' [,'format_string' ...]
| TRACE [=] integer
| { MAXPIECESIZE [=] integer
  | RATE [=] integer } [ K | M | G ]
| MAXOPENFILES [=] integer
| SEND 'command'
}
```

Oracle8i syntax

```
allocOperand :=
{ PARMS [=]'channel_parms'
| CONNECT [=] connectStringSpec
| DEBUG [=] integer
| FORMAT [=]'format_string' [,'format_string' ...]
| TRACE [=] integer
}
```

Keywords

PARMS

Specifies parameters for a nondisk device that has been allocated.

CONNECT connectStringSpec

Indicates an alternate database that will be the target of backup and restore operations.

DEBUG integer

Logs debugging information to an output file for backup, copy, or restore commands that use the channel.

TRACE integer

Specifies the level of trace information that is logged to an output file. The exact meaning of the integer is defined by the media management software.

MAXPIECESIZE integer

Specifies the maximum size for a backup piece.

RATE integer

Specifies the maximum number of bytes that RMAN will read per channel in bytes, kilobytes (K), megabytes (M), or gigabytes (G).

MAXOPENFILES integer

Specifies the maximum number of files that RMAN is allowed to have open at any given time.

SEND 'command'

Sends a vendor-specific command to all of the allocated channels.

ALTER DATABASE

This command is analogous to the SQL ALTER DATABASE command. It is used to mount and open a database from the RMAN prompt. This command can be executed from within the RUN command or directly from the RMAN prompt.

Syntax

```
{ ALTER DATABASE { MOUNT | OPEN [RESETLOGS] }
| { MOUNT | OPEN [RESETLOGS] DATABASE };
```

Keywords

MOUNT
  Mounts the database without opening it.

OPEN
  Opens the database.

RESETLOGS
  Resets the online redo logs to start at sequence number 1. If the RMAN ALTER DATABASE command is used, the target database is automatically reset within the catalog. If you use the SQL*Plus command, you must execute the RMAN RESET DATABASE command in order to reset the target database within the catalog.

archivelogRecordSpecifier

This clause allows flexibility in specifying the archived redo log files that will be included in backup, restore, and maintenance operations.

Syntax

```
ARCHIVELOG
   { ALL
   | LIKE 'string_pattern'
   | archlogRange
     [LIKE 'string_pattern' [THREAD [=] integer]]
   }

archlogRange for Oracle9i :=
{ { { UNTIL TIME | FROM TIME } [=] 'date_string'
  | { TIME BETWEEN 'date_string' AND
    | FROM TIME [=] 'date_string' UNTIL TIME [=]
    }
    'date_string'
  | UNTIL SCN [=] integer
  | SCN BETWEEN integer AND integer
  | FROM SCN [=] integer [UNTIL SCN [=] integer]
  }
  [THREAD [=] integer]
  | { UNTIL SEQUENCE [=] integer
  | FROM SEQUENCE [=] integer [UNTIL SEQUENCE [=] integer]
  | SEQUENCE [BETWEEN integer AND] integer
```

```
    }
    [THREAD [=] integer]
}

archlogRange for Oracle8i :=
{ { UNTIL TIME | FROM TIME } [=]'date_string'
  | FROM TIME [=]'date_string' UNTIL TIME [=]'date_string'
  | UNTIL SCN [=]integer
  | FROM SCN [=] integer [UNTIL SCN [=] integer]
  | UNTIL LOGSEQ [=] integer [THREAD [=] integer]
  | FROM LOGSEQ [=] integer [UNTIL LOGSEQ [=] integer]
    [THREAD [=] integer]
}
```

Keywords

ALL

Specifies that all logs should be included in the specified operation

LIKE 'string_pattern'

Includes those logs that match the specified pattern

archlogRange

Includes those logs that match specified criteria for time, SCN, or sequence number

THREAD integer

Specifies a redo thread and is used only with Oracle Real Application Clusters

---

BACKUP

Creates a backup of a database of a physical component such as a database file, of an archived redo log file, or of a logical component such as a tablespace. For Oracle8i, this command must be executed from within the RUN command.

```
Oracle9i SyntaxBACKUP [ FULL | INCREMENTAL LEVEL [=]
integer ]
[backupOperand [backupOperand ...]]
backupSpec [backupSpec]...
[PLUS ARCHIVELOG
[backupSpecOperand [backupSpecOperand ...]]];
```

```
backupOperand :=
{ FORMAT [=] 'format_string' [, 'format_string' ...]
| CHANNEL [']channel_id[']
| CUMULATIVE
| MAXSETSIZE [=] integer [ K | M | G ]
| FILESPERSET [=] integer
| PARMS [=] 'channel_parms'
| POOL [=] integer
| TAG [=] [']tag_name[']
| keepOption
| SKIP { OFFLINE | READONLY | INACCESSIBLE }
| NOEXCLUDE
| PROXY [ONLY]
| VALIDATE
| FORCE
| DISKRATIO [=] integer
| NOT BACKED UP [SINCE TIME [=] 'date_string']
| NOCHECKSUM
| CHECK LOGICAL
| COPIES [=] integer
| DEVICE TYPE deviceSpecifier
}

backupSpec :=
[(]
{ BACKUPSET
  { { ALL | completedTimeSpec }
  | primary_key [, primary_key ...]
  }
| DATAFILE datafileSpec [, datafileSpec ...]
| DATAFILECOPY 'filename' [, 'filename' ...]
| DATAFILECOPY TAG [=] [']tag_name['] [,
    [']tag_name['] ...]
| TABLESPACE [']tablespace_name[']
    [, [']tablespace_name['] ...]
| DATABASE
| archivelogRecordSpecifier
| CURRENT CONTROLFILE [FOR STANDBY]
| CONTROLFILECOPY 'filename'
}
[backupSpecOperand [backupSpecOperand]...]
[)]

backupSpecOperand :=
{ FORMAT [=] 'format_string' [, 'format_string' ...]
| CHANNEL [']channel_id[']
```

```
 | MAXSETSIZE [=] integer [ K | M | G ]
 | FILESPERSET [=] integer
 | PARMS [=]'channel_parms'
 | POOL [=] integer
 | TAG [=] [']tag_name[']
 | keepOption
 | SKIP { OFFLINE | READONLY | INACCESSIBLE }
 | NOEXCLUDE
 | FORCE
 | DISKRATIO [=] integer
 | NOT BACKED UP [SINCE TIME [=] 'date_string']
 | INCLUDE CURRENT CONTROLFILE [FOR STANDBY]
 | DELETE [ALL] INPUT
 }
```

Oracle8i syntax

```
BACKUP [ FULL | INCREMENTAL LEVEL [=] integer ]
[backupOperand [backupOperand]...]
backupSpec [backupSpec];

backupOperand :=
{ FORMAT [=] 'format_string' [, 'format_string' ...]
| CHANNEL [']channel_id[']
| CUMULATIVE
| FILESPERSET [=] integer
| PARMS [=] 'channel_parms'
| POOL [=] integer
| TAG [=] [']tag_name[']
| keepOption
| SKIP { OFFLINE | READONLY | INACCESSIBLE }
| PROXY [ONLY]
| DISKRATIO [=] integer
| NOCHECKSUM
| CHECK LOGICAL
| SETSIZE [=] integer
}

backupSpec :=
[()
{ DATAFILE datafileSpec [, datafileSpec ...]
| DATAFILECOPY 'filename' [, 'filename' ...]
| DATAFILECOPY TAG [=] [']tag_name['] [,\
  [']tag_name['] ...]
| TABLESPACE [']tablespace_name['] [,\
  [']tablespace_name['] ...]
| DATABASE
```

```
| archivelogRecordSpecifier
| CURRENT CONTROLFILE
| CONTROLFILECOPY 'filename'
}
[backupSpecOperand [backupSpecOperand]...]
[)]

backupSpecOperand :=
{ FORMAT [=] 'format_string' [,'format_string' ...]
| CHANNEL [']channel_id[']
| FILESPERSET [=] integer
| PARMS [=] 'channel_parms'
| POOL [=] integer
| TAG [=] [']tag_name[']
| SKIP { OFFLINE | READONLY | INACCESSIBLE }
| DISKRATIO [=] integer
| INCLUDE CURRENT CONTROLFILE
| DELETE INPUT
| SETSIZE [=] integer
}
```

Keywords

CURRENT CONTROLFILE [FOR STANDBY]

Indicates that the current control file should also be backed up. If the FOR STANDBY option is used, a control file will be created that can be used for the creation of a standby database.

CUMULATIVE

Causes RMAN to back up only those blocks that have changed since the most recent backup taken at a prior level.

MAXSETSIZE integer

Limits a backup set to a specified size. You may specify the size in bytes, kilobytes (K), megabytes (M), or gigabytes (G).

FILESPERSET integer

Limits a backup set to the specified number of files.

PARMS 'channel_parms'

Sends O/S-specific information to the O/S layer each time a backup piece is created.

POOL
> Specifies a media management pool where the backup should be kept. This is used in conjunction with the media management software.

SKIP
> Skips datafiles that are read-only, offline, or inaccessible.

NOEXCLUDE
> Overrides default settings that have previously been established with CONFIGURE EXCLUDE.

PROXY
> Allows the media manager to make decisions on when and how data is to be transferred.

VALIDATE
> Validates files for physical and logical errors.

FORCE
> Allows the backup to ignore optimization settings specified with CONFIGURE.

DISKRATIO integer
> Load balances the backup across disks.

NOT BACKED UP [SINCE TIME 'date_string']
> Backs up those files that have not been backed up or have not been backed up since a specific date and time.

NO CHECKSUM
> Prevents block checksums from being computed.

COPIES integer
> Specifies the number of backup copies to be created. The default is 1.

DELETE
> Deletes the backup set, datafile copy, or archived log input file upon successful completion of the backup.

Examples

Please see "Backing Up a Datafile," earlier in this book, for examples of the BACKUP command.

BLOCKRECOVER (Oracle9i only)

This command allows for a fine-grained level of recovery by specifying a small list of corrupt blocks rather than an entire datafile.

Syntax

```
BLOCKRECOVER
[DEVICE TYPE deviceSpecifier [, deviceSpecifier]...]
blockSpec [blockSpec]... [blockOption [blockOption]...];

blockSpec :=
{ DATAFILE datafileSpec BLOCK integer [, integer ...]
| TABLESPACE tablespace_name DBA integer [, integer ...]
| CORRUPTION LIST
}

blockOption :=
{ FROM { BACKUPSET | DATAFILECOPY }
| FROM TAG [=] [']tag_name[']
| RESTORE untilClause
}
```

Keywords

BLOCK integer
Specifies the block(s) that requires recovery

DBA
Specifies the data block address of a block to recover

CORRUPTION LIST
Recovers those blocks that are listed in the dictionary views V$COPY_CORRUPTION and V$BACKUP_CORRUPTION

FROM
Specifies that restoration should be either from a backup set or a datafile copy

FROM TAG tag_name
Specifies the backup set that needs to be restored, and from which you want to perform block level recovery

RESTORE untilClause
Specifies that backup sets created before a given time are to be restored

CATALOG

Adds information pertaining to user-managed COPY commands to the recovery catalog.

Syntax

```
CATALOG { CONTROLFILECOPY | DATAFILECOPY | ARCHIVELOG }
   'filename' [, 'filename' ...]
[TAG [=] [']tag_name ['] | LEVEL [=] integer ]
[ TAG [=] [']tag_name['] | LEVEL [=] integer ]...;
```

Keywords

CONTROLFILECOPY `'filename'`
> Specifies the filename of the copied control file that should be added to the recovery catalog

DATEFILECOPY `'filename'`
> Specifies the filename of the copied datafile that should be added to the recovery catalog

ARCHIVELOG `'filename'`
> Specifies the filename of an archived redo log file that should be added to the recovery catalog

TAG tag_name
> Specifies a tag name that will be assigned to the file within the recovery catalog

LEVEL integer
> Specifies that the file copy should be recorded within the recovery catalog with the specified increment level

Example

The following example adds information to the recovery catalog on a COPY command that occurred just when a connection to the target database had been established. First, here's an example of a user-managed COPY command:

```
RMAN> run {
2> allocate channel d1 type disk;
3> copy datafile '/d02/oradata/brdstn/users_01.dbf'
4> to '/d99/users_01.dbf'; }
```

Once a connection to the recovery catalog has been established, the information about the COPY command can be registered:

```
RMAN> catalog datafilecopy '/d99/users_01.dbf' level 0;
```

CHANGE

Enables you to perform maintenance on backup sets or their associated backup pieces. Maintenance can take the form of:

- Changing the status repository records for backup sets and backup pieces
- Deleting backup pieces from disk or tape media, which would also remove the associated records from the target database's control files and from the optional recovery catalog

Oracle9i syntax

```
CHANGE
    { { BACKUP | COPY } [OF listObj]
      [mntQualifer [mntQualifer]...]
    | recordSpec
      [DEVICE TYPE deviceSpecifier [, deviceSpecifier]...]
    }
    { AVAILABLE | UNAVAILABLE | UNCATALOG | keepOption }
    [DEVICE TYPE deviceSpecifier [, deviceSpecifier]...];
```

Oracle8i syntax

```
CHANGE
    { ARCHIVELOG
      { primary_key [, primary_key...]
      | 'filename' [,'filename' ...] }
    | arhivelogRecordSpecifier
    | BACKUPPIECE { 'media_handle' [,'media_handle' ...]
                  | primary_key [, primary_key ...]
                  | TAG [=] [']tag_name['] }
    | BACKUPSET primary_key [, primary_key ...]
    | { CONTROLFILECOPY | DATAFILECOPY }
      { primary_key [, primary_key ...]
      | 'filename' [,'filename' ...]
      | TAG [=] ['] tag_name ['] [, ['] tag_name
          ['] ... ] }
    | PROXY { 'media_handle' [,'media_handle' ...]
            | primary_key [, primary_key ...]
```

```
          | TAG [=] [']tag_name['] }
}
{ DELETE | AVAILABLE | UNAVAILABLE
| UNCATAOG | CROSSCHECK };
```

Keywords

AVAILABLE

Changes the status of backups or copies to AVAILABLE.

UNAVAILABLE

Changes the status of backups or copies to UNAVAILABLE.
Backups marked as UNAVAILABLE are not used by RMAN.
Therefore, a subsequent recovery operation will look for a
prior available backup.

UNCATALOG

Deletes records associated with datafile copies and archived
redo log files from the catalog, and marks that information as
DELETED in the target database's control file.

Examples

The following example deletes the backup piece represented by
the file named *1ccn3ed4_1_1*:

```
RMAN> allocate channel for maintenance type disk;
RMAN> change backuppiece '/d99/backups/1ccn3ed4_1_1'
2> delete;
RMAN> release channel;
```

This next example marks a backup set as unavailable:

```
RMAN> allocate channel for maintenance type disk;
RMAN> change backupset 1180 unavailable;
RMAN> release channel;
```

completedTimeSpec

Specifies the completion time of a backup.

Syntax

```
completedTimeSpec :=
COMPLETED
{ AFTER [=]
```

```
| BETWEEN 'date_string' AND
| BEFORE [=] } 'date_string'
```

Keywords

AFTER 'date_string'
Specifies a time after which a backup or copy occurred

BETWEEN 'date_string' AND 'date_string'
Specifies a date range during which backups or copies occurred

BEFORE 'date_string'
Specifies a time before a backup or copy occurred

CONFIGURE (Oracle9i only)

Establishes settings that remain persistent for an RMAN session.

Syntax

```
CONFIGURE
{ configureDevice
| configureBackup
| { AUXNAME FOR DATAFILE datafileSpec
  | SNAPSHOT CONTROLFILE NAME
  }
  { TO 'filename' | CLEAR }
| configureCtlfile
};

configureDevice :=
{ DEFAULT DEVICE TYPE { TO deviceSpecifier | CLEAR }
| DEVICE TYPE deviceSpecifier
  { PARALLELISM integer | CLEAR }
| [AUXILIARY] CHANNEL [integer]
  DEVICE TYPE deviceSpecifier { allocOperand | CLEAR }
}

configureBackup :=
{ RETENTION POLICY { TO { RECOVERY WINDOW OF integer DAYS
                        | REDUNDANCY [=] integer
                        | NONE
                        }
                    | CLEAR
                }
```

```
   | MAXSETSIZE { TO { integer [ K | M | G ]
                     | UNLIMITED
                     }
              | CLEAR
          }
   | { ARCHIVELOG | DATAFILE }
     BACKUP COPIES FOR DEVICE TYPE deviceSpecifier
     { TO integer | CLEAR }
   | BACKUP OPTIMIZATION { ON | OFF | CLEAR }
   | EXCLUDE FOR TABLESPACE tablespace_name [CLEAR]
   }

   configureCtlfile :=
   CONTROLFILE AUTOBACKUP
   { ON
   | OFF
   | CLEAR
   | FORMAT FOR DEVICE TYPE
       deviceSpecifier { TO 'format_string' | CLEAR }
   }
```

Keywords

SNAPSHOT CONTROLFILE NAME
    Defines the name and path of the snapshot control file. The
    default is platform-specific. In Unix, the default is
    $ORACLE_HOME/dbs.

DEFAULT DEVICE TYPE
    Specifies the default media type as disk or tape.

DEVICE TYPE deviceSpecifier
    Specifies the device type for use with automatic channels and
    establishes the degree of parallelism, which is the number of
    channels that will be allocated and used. The default degree
    of parallelism is 1.

PARALLELISM integer
    Establishes the number of automatic channels for the device.

RETENTION POLICY
    Defines a retention policy whereby RMAN flags backup sets
    as obsolete so that they can subsequently be manually
    deleted.

RECOVERY WINDOW OF
> Defines a recovery window based on SYSDATE minus a specified number of days. Backups taken prior to the computed date are marked as obsolete.

REDUNDANCY
> Defines the redundant number of backups or copies that RMAN should not consider as obsolete. The default is 1.

MAXSETSIZE integer
> Defines the maximum size of a backup piece for each channel in bytes, kilobytes (K), megabytes (M), or gigabytes (G). The default value is UNLIMITED.

CONTROLFILE AUTOBACKUP
> Specifies whether *autobackup* of the control file is enabled. The default is OFF.

FORMAT FOR DEVICE TYPE
> Defines the filename and location for the control file. The default is %F (see Table 1-1).

CLEAR
> Reestablishes the default value.

Example

The following example establishes the default-device type as disk and defines the format to use when naming backup pieces:

```
RMAN> CONFIGURE CHANNEL DEVICE TYPE DISK FORMAT
2> '/d99/rmanback/rman_%U.bus';
```

CONNECT

Establishes a connection to a target, catalog, or an auxiliary database to perform backup, restore, or recovery operations.

Syntax

```
{ CONNECT TARGET [connectStringSpec] [;]
| { CONNECT CATALOG | CONNECT AUXILIARY }
connectStringSpec [;]
}
```

Examples

The following example connects to an Oracle8*i* target database without using the optional recovery catalog:

```
$> rman target / nocatalog
```

This example connects to both a target database and a recovery catalog:

```
$> rman target / catalog rman901/secret@rman_catalog
```

connectStringSpec

Specifies the necessary information for connecting to a target, catalog, or auxiliary database.

Syntax

```
['][userid][/[password]][@net_service_name][']
```

COPY

Creates image file copies of database files. For Oracle8*i*, this command must be executed from within the RUN command.

Syntax

```
COPY [copyOption [copyOption]...]
{ copyInputfile TO
  { AUXNAME | 'filename' [copyOption [copyOption]...] }
  [, copy_inputfile TO
  { AUXNAME | 'filename' [copyOption [copyOption]...] }
  ]...
| (copyInputfile TO
  { AUXNAME | 'filename' [copyOption [copyOption]...] }
  )
  [(copy_inputfile TO
   { AUXNAME | 'filename' [copyOption [copyOption]...] }
   )
  ]...
};

Oracle9i copyOption :=
{ TAG [=] [']tag_name[']
| LEVEL [=] integer
```

```
| NOCHECKSUM
| CHECK LOGICAL
| keepOption
}

Oracle9i copyInputFile :=
{ DATAFILE datafileSpec
| DATAFILECOPY
  { 'filename' | TAG [=] [']tag_name['] }
| ARCHIVELOG 'filename'
| CURRENT CONTROLFILE [FOR STANDBY]
| CONTROLFILECOPY
  { 'filename' | TAG [=] [']tag_name['] }
}

Oracle8i copyOption :=
{ TAG [=] [']tag_name[']
| LEVEL [=] integer
| NOCHECKSUM
| CHECK LOGICAL
}

Oracle8i copyInputFile :=
{ DATAFILE datafileSpec
| DATAFILECOPY
  { 'filename' | TAG [=] [']tag_name['] }
| ARCHIVELOG 'filename'
| CURRENT CONTROLFILE
| CONTROLFILECOPY
  { 'filename' | TAG [=] [']tag_name['] }
}
```

Keywords

AUXNAME
Specifies that the result of the COPY command is an alternate name for a file that was previously defined through the SET command

NO CHECKSUM
Prevents block checksums from being computed

CREATE CATALOG

Creates a schema within a recovery catalog database.

Syntax

```
CREATE CATALOG [TABLESPACE [']tablespace_name[']][;]
```

Keywords

TABLESPACE tablespace_name

Specifies the tablespace to use for the recovery catalog objects. By default, the catalog schema owner's default tablespace is used.

Example

```
RMAN> create catalog;
```

CREATE SCRIPT

Creates and stores a script in the catalog repository.

Syntax

```
CREATE SCRIPT [']script_name[']
{
   { backupCommands
     | restoreCommands
     | maintenanceCommands
     | miscellaneousCommands
   }
   [ backupCommands
     | restoreCommands
     | maintenancecommands
     | miscellaneousCommands

     ...
   ]
}

backupCommands :=
{ BACKUP
| COPY
}

restoreCommands :=
{ REPLICATE
| RESTORE
| RECOVER
| BLOCKRECOVER
```

```
| DUPLICATE
| SWITCH
}

maintenanceCommands :=
{ CATALOG
| CHANGE
| CONFIGURE
| CROSSCHECK
| DELETE
| VALIDATE
| REPORT
| DELETE
| SHOW
}

miscellaneousCommands :=
{ ALLOCATE
| ALTERDATABASE
| BEGINLINE
| DEBUG
| EXECUTESCRIPT
| HOST
| RELEASE
| RESYNC
| SEND
| SET
| SHUTDOWN
| SQL
| STARTUP
}
```

Examples

See the section "Stored Catalog Scripts" earlier in this book.

CROSSCHECK

Determines whether a backup set and its related pieces still exist on media. If a backup piece exists in the location recorded in the control file of the target database or in the optional recovery catalog, its status is marked as AVAILABLE. If it is not at the specified location, it is marked as EXPIRED.

Oracle9i syntax

```
CROSSCHECK
    { { BACKUP | COPY }
      [OF listObj] [mntQualifer [mntQualifer]...]
    | recordSpec
      [DEVICE TYPE deviceSpecifier [, deviceSpecifier]...]
    };
```

Oracle8i syntax

```
CROSSCHECK BACKUP
    [ OF listObj ]
    [ checkOptions [ checkOptions...]];

checkOptions :=
{ TAG [=] [']tag_name[']
| completedTimeSpec }
```

Example

In the following example, the existence of all backup sets are
verified:

```
RMAN> allocate channel for maintenance type disk;
RMAN> crosscheck backup;
RMAN> release channel;
```

In the following example, the backup pieces that contain the
SYSTEM tablespace are validated for all backup sets:

```
RMAN> allocate channel for maintenance type disk;
RMAN> crosscheck backup of tablespace system;
RMAN> release channel;
```

---

datafileSpec

Specifies a datafile by its fully qualified filename or by its file
number.

Syntax

```
datafileSpec := { 'filename' | file_number}
```

DELETE

For Oracle9*i*, this command deletes the physical files associated with backup sets and datafile copies, updates their status in the control file, and removes their information from the optional recovery catalog (if one is used).

In Oracle8*i* and Oracle9*i*, backups are flagged as EXPIRED if they cannot be found at their recorded location. Deletion of EXPIRED backups removes their information from the control file and from the optional recovery catalog (if one is used).

Oracle9i syntax

```
DELETE [NOPROMPT]
    { [EXPIRED]
      { { BACKUP | COPY }
        [OF listObj] [mntQualifer [mntQualifer]...]
      | recordSpec
        [DEVICE TYPE deviceSpecifier [, deviceSpecifier]...
]
      }
    | OBSOLETE [obsoleteOpersList]
      [DEVICE TYPE (deviceSpecifier [, deviceSpecifier]...]
    };
```

Oracle8i syntax

```
DELETE EXPIRED BACKUP
    [ OF listObj ]
    [ deleteOptions [ deleteOptions...]];

deleteOptions :=
    { TAG [=] [']tag_name[']
    | completedTimeSpec }
```

Keywords

NOPROMPT
> Deletes the specified files without confirmation

EXPIRED
> Deletes those files that have been marked as EXPIRED in the catalog

---

OBSOLETE
Deletes those files that are no longer needed for recovery

Example

The following Oracle8*i* example removes the records associated with EXPIRED backups from the control files of the target database and the optional recovery catalog (if used):

```
RMAN> allocate channel for maintenance type disk;
RMAN> crosscheck backup;
...
RMAN-08074: crosschecked backup piece: found to be
  'EXPIRED'
RMAN-08517: backup piece handle=/d99/rman/brdstn/rman_lo_
  BRDSTN_Occv8lck_1_1.bus recid=12 stamp=435443094

RMAN> delete expired backup of database;
RMAN-08517: backup piece handle=/d99/rman/brdstn/rman_lo_
  BRDSTN_Occv8lck_1_1.bus recid=12 stamp=435443094
RMAN-08073: deleted backup piece
```

This Oracle 9*i* example deletes the physical files assocated with the backup and removes their associated records from the control files of the target database and the optional recovery catalog (if used):

```
RMAN> delete backup of database;
List of Backup Pieces
BP Key  BS Key  Pc# Cp# Status      Device Type Piece Name
------- ------- --- --- ----------- ----------- ----------
25      25      1   1   AVAILABLE   DISK        /d99/rman_
                                                Oucv8npu_
                                                1_1.bus
Do you really want to delete the above objects (enter YES
  or NO)? YES
deleted backup piece
backup piece handle=/d99/rman_Oscv8npr_1_1.bus
  recid=26 stamp=435445566
```

DELETE SCRIPT

Removes a stored script from a recovery catalog.

Syntax

```
DELETE SCRIPT [']script_name['];
```

deviceSpecifier

Specifies the storage type that will be used in a backup or a copy command.

Syntax

```
{ DISK | [']media_device['] }
```

DROP CATALOG

Drops all objects associated with the recovery catalog schema.

Syntax

```
DROP CATALOG[;]
```

DUPLICATE

Creates a duplicate database, or a standby database, from the backups of a target database. For Oracle8*i*, this command must be executed from within the RUN command.

Oracle9i syntax

```
DUPLICATE TARGET DATABASE
   { TO [']database_name[']
     [ [dupOptionList] [dupOptionList ...] ]
   | FOR STANDBY [ [dupsbyOptionList]
        [dupOptionList ...] ]
   };

dupOptionList :=
{ LOGFILE logSpec [, logSpec]...
| NOFILENAMECHECK
| SKIP READONLY
| DEVICE TYPE deviceSpecifier [, deviceSpecifier ...]
| PFILE [=] [']filename[']
}
```

```
logSpec :=
{ 'filename' [SIZE integer [ K | M ] [REUSE]
| GROUP integer ('filename' [, 'filename' ...])
   [SIZE integer [ K | M ] [REUSE] }

dupsbyOptionList :=
{ DORECOVER | NOFILENAMECHECK }
```

Oracle8i syntax

```
DUPLICATE TARGET DATABASE TO [']database_name[']
   [ LOGFILE logSpec [, logSpec ...]
   [ NOFILENAMECHECK ]
   [ SKIP READONLY ];

logSpec :=
   { 'filename' [SIZE integer [ K | M ] [REUSE]
   | GROUP integer ('filename' [, 'filename' ...])
      [SIZE integer [ K | M ] [REUSE] }
```

Keywords

NOFILENAMECHECK

Causes RMAN not to check to see if the target database filenames are the same as those in the duplicate database. Use
this option only when duplicating a database to a different
host, in which case it's OK for the directory and filenames to
be the same.

PFILE

Specifies the location of the parameter file for the duplicated
database. RMAN uses the parameter file at this location, which
you must have previously created, to start the duplicated database. This option must be used if the location of the parameter
file is not in the default location (*$ORACLE_HOME/dbs*).

DORECOVER

Causes RMAN to recover the standby database after creating
it. Archived redo logs will be applied as necessary.

EXECUTE SCRIPT

Executes a script that has been stored in the repository catalog.
This command must be executed from within the braces of the
RUN command.

Syntax

```
EXECUTE SCRIPT [']script_name['];
```

Examples

This example shows how to execute a script named *full_back*:

```
RMAN> run {execute script full_back;}
```

EXIT

Exits the RMAN utility.

Syntax

```
EXIT[;]
```

HOST

Initiates an O/S shell whereby O/S commands can be executed.

Syntax

```
HOST [{' | "}command{' | "}];
```

Examples

Use HOST by itself to get to an O/S shell prompt. Exiting the shell returns control to the RMAN session.

```
RMAN> host;
$> ls -lt
...
$> exit
RMAN>
```

The following example passes a command as a parameter in order to execute that command and return directly to RMAN:

```
RMAN> host 'ls -lt';

total 2
-rwx------ 1 oracle dba 186 Jul 2 20:17 full_bck.ksh
host command complete

RMAN>
```

keepOption (Oracle9i only)

Specifies that a backup or copy is to be considered exempt from a specified retention policy.

Syntax

```
{ KEEP { UNTIL TIME [=] 'date_string' | FOREVER } { LOGS |
    NOLOGS }
| NOKEEP
}
```

Keywords

UNTIL TIME 'date_string'
Specifies that the backup or copy should be kept until the specified date.

FOREVER
Specifies that the backup will be kept indefinitely. This requires the use of a recovery catalog because the backup or copy will never expire.

LOGS
Keeps all archived redo log files associated with a backup or copy.

NOLOGS
Specifies that archived redo log files associated with a backup or copy will not be kept. Consequently, the database can be restored only to the point in time when the backup or copy was made.

LIST

Produces detailed lists of backups or image copies.

Oracle9i syntax

```
LIST
    { INCARNATION [OF DATABASE [[']database_name[']]]
    | [EXPIRED]
      { listObjectSpec
        [ mntQualifer | RECOVERABLE [untilClause] ]
        [ mntQualifer | RECOVERABLE [untilClause] ]...
```

```
      | recordSpec
      }
    };

listObjectSpec :=
{ BACKUP [OF listObj] [listBackupOption]
| COPY [OF listObj]
}

listBackupOption :=
[ [BY BACKUP] [VERBOSE]
| SUMMARY
| BY { BACKUP SUMMARY | FILE }
]
```

Oracle8i syntax

```
LIST
    { INCARNATION [OF DATABASE [ [']database_name['] ] ]
    | { BACKUP | COPY } [OF listObj]
      [ listOptions [listOptions ...] ];

listOptions :=
{ { TAG [=] [']tag_name[']
  | completedTimeSpec }
| RECOVERABLE [ untilClause ]
| DEVICE TYPE deviceSpecifier [, deviceSpecifier ...]
| LIKE 'string_pattern' }
```

Keywords

EXPIRED

Lists backup sets that have been marked as EXPIRED in the control files of the target database of the recovery catalog

BY BACKUP

Lists backup sets and their contents

VERBOSE

Lists detailed backup set information

SUMMARY

Lists a one-line summary for backup sets or files and summary information for backup sets or files

---

Examples

To produce a detailed listing of all backups:

```
RMAN> list backup;
```

To produce a detailed listing of all backup sets containing the SYSTEM tablespace:

```
RMAN> list backup of tablespace system;
```

To show information on backed-up archived redo logs:

```
RMAN> list backup of archivelog all;
```

The following Oracle9i example lists summary backup information for the tablespace SYSTEM:

```
RMAN>  list backup of tablespace system summary;

List of Backups
===============
Key  TY LV S Device Type Completion Time #Pieces #Copies
Tag
---- -- -- - ----------- --------------- ------- -------
1179 B  F  X DISK        07-JUL-01       1       1
1248 B  F  A DISK        09-JUL-01       1       1
```

listObj

A subclause specifying the database elements that will be included in backup, restore, and maintenance operations.

Syntax

```
ListObj :=
{ DATAFILE datafileSpec [, datafileSpec ...]
| TABLESPACE [']tablespace_name[']
  [, [']tablespace_name['] ...]
| archivelogRecordSpecifier
| DATABASE [SKIP TABLESPACE
  [']tablespace_name['] [, [']tablespace_name[']]...]
| CONTROLFILE
}
[ DATAFILE datafileSpec [, datafileSpec]...
| TABLESPACE [']tablespace_name[']
  [, [']tablespace_name['] ...]
```

```
| archivelogRecordSpecifier
| DATABASE [SKIP TABLESPACE
  [']tablespace_name['] [, [']tablespace_name[']]...]
| CONTROLFILE
]...
```

mntQualifer (Oracle9i only)

A subclause allowing for additional options to be included when performing maintenance operations on database files and archived redo log files.

Syntax

```
{ TAG [=] [']tag_name[']
| completedTimeSpec
| LIKE 'string_pattern'
| DEVICE TYPE deviceSpecifier [, deviceSpecifier ...]
}
```

obsoleteOpersList (Oracle9i only)

A subclause used to specify those backups that can be considered obsolete.

Syntax

```
obsoleteOpersList :=
{ REDUNDANCY [=] integer
| RECOVERY WINDOW OF integer DAYS | ORPHAN }
[ REDUNDANCY [=] integer
| RECOVERY WINDOW OF integer DAYS | ORPHAN ]...
```

Keywords

REDUNDANCY integer
  Specifies a number of redundant backups or copies that must be kept available

ORPHAN
  Indicates that a backup is obsolete

PRINT SCRIPT

Displays a script that is stored in the repository catalog.

Syntax

```
PRINT SCRIPT [']script_name['];
```

Example

The following example displays a script that has been stored in the recovery catalog:

```
RMAN> print script full_back;

printing stored script: full_back
{
    allocate channel d1 type disk;
    backup full format '/d0102/backup/rman_%d_%U.bus'
        database;
}
```

QUIT (Oracle9i only)

Exits the RMAN utility.

Syntax

```
QUIT[;]
```

RecordSpec (Oracle9i only)

A subclause used to specify types of objects on which to operate when performing maintenance.

Syntax

```
RecordSpec :=
{ { BACKUPPIECE | PROXY }
  { 'media_handle' [, 'media_handle' ...]
  | primary_key [, primary_key ...]
  | TAG [=] [']tag_name[']
  }
```

```
| BACKUPSET primary_key [, primary_key ...]
| { CONTROLFILECOPY | DATAFILECOPY }
  { { primary_key [, primary_key ...]
    | 'filename' [, 'filename' ...]
    }
  | TAG [=] [']tag_name['] [, [']tag_name['] ...]
  }
| ARCHIVELOG
  { primary_key [, primary_key ...]
  | 'filename' [, 'filename' ...]
  }
| archivelogRecordSpecifier
}
```

Keywords

BACKUPPIECE

Specifies the physical backup piece by either its filename, primary key, or tag name

PROXY

Specifies a proxy copy by its filename, primary key, or tag name

CONTROLFILECOPY

Specifies a control file copy by its filename, primary key, or tag name

DATAFILECOPY

Specifies a datafile copy by its filename, primary key, or tag name

---

RECOVER

Recovers a database or one of its physical components. During the recovery process, either incremental backups (the first choice) or archived redo log files are applied to recover the datafiles. For Oracle8i, this command must be executed from within the RUN command.

Oracle9i syntax

```
RECOVER [DEVICE TYPE deviceSpecifier
    [, deviceSpecifier]...]
recoverObject [recoverOptionList];
```

```
recoverObject :=
{ DATABASE
  [ untilClause
  | [untilClause] SKIP [FOREVER] TABLESPACE
    [']tablespace_name['] [, [']tablespace_name['] ...]
  ]
| TABLESPACE [']tablespace_name[']
  [, [']tablespace_name['] ...]
| DATAFILE datafileSpec [, datafileSpec ...]
}

recoverOptionList :=
{ DELETE ARCHIVELOG
| CHECK READONLY
| NOREDO
| CHECK LOGICAL
| { FROM TAG | ARCHIVELOG TAG } [=] [']tag_name[']
}
[, { DELETE ARCHIVELOG
   | CHECK READONLY
   | NOREDO
   | CHECK LOGICAL
   | { FROM TAG | ARCHIVELOG TAG } [=] [']tag_name[']
   }
]...
```

Oracle8i syntax

```
RECOVER recoverObject [recoverOptionList];

RecoverOptionList :=
{ DELETE ARCHIVELOG
| CHECK READONLY
| NOREDO
| CHECK LOGICAL
}
[, { DELETE ARCHIVELOG
   | CHECK READONLY
   | NOREDO
   | CHECK LOGICAL
   }
] ...
```

Keywords

DELETE ARCHIVELOG
> Removes archived redo log files that are no longer necessary.

CHECK READONLY
> Excludes read-only tablespaces from the recovery process if their datafiles files are current.

NOREDO
> Forces the recovery to be performed using only incremental backups. No archived redo log files are applied. This option is valid when recovering a database operating in *noarchivelog* mode.

Examples

For examples, see "Restoring Files" earlier in this book.

REGISTER

Registers a target database with a repository catalog. You must connect to the catalog and to the target that you wish to register before issuing this command.

Syntax

```
REGISTER DATABASE;
```

RELEASE CHANNEL

Releases a channel that has been allocated for I/O purposes. Once allocated, channels remain open until the job has finished execution, or they have specifically been released. For the latter, you can use this command to release a specified channel while RMAN maintains a connection to the target database. For Oracle8*i*, this command must be executed from within the RUN command.

Syntax

```
RELEASE CHANNEL [']channel_id['];
```

Example

In the following example, a channel is allocated for maintenance, a crosscheck operation is performed, and the channel is then manually released:

```
RMAN> run {
2> allocate channel d1 type disk;
3> backup incremental level 0 database;
4> release channel d1;
5> }
```

releaseForMaint

Releases a channel that has been allocated for maintenance purposes.

Syntax

```
RELEASE CHANNEL;
```

Example

The following command allocates a channel for maintenance purposes, changes a backup set's status, and releases the channel:

```
RMAN> allocate channel for maintenance type disk;
RMAN> change backupset 1180 unavailable;
RMAN> release channel;
```

REPLACE SCRIPT

Replaces a script that has been stored in the repository catalog. If the script to be replaced does not exist, it is created.

Syntax

```
REPLACE SCRIPT [']script_name[']
{
 { backupCommands
 | restoreCommands
 | maintenanceCommands
 | miscellaneousCommands
 }
```

```
[ backupCommands
| restoreCommands
| maintenanceCommands
| miscellaneousCommands
]...
}

backupCommands :=
{ BACKUP
| COPY
}

restoreCommands :=
{ REPLICATE
| RESTORE
| RECOVER
| BLOCKRECOVER
| DUPLICATE
| SWITCH
}

maintenanceCommands :=
{ CATALOG
| CHANGE
| CONFIGURE
| CROSSCHECK
| DELETE
| VALIDATE
| REPORT
| DELETE
| SHOW
}

miscellaneousCommands :=
{ ALLOCATE
| ALTERDATABASE
| beginLine
| DEBUG
| executeScript
| HOST
| RELEASE
| RESYNC
| SEND
| SET
| SHUTDOWN
| SQL
```

```
| STARTUP
}
```

Examples

See "Stored Catalog Scripts" earlier in this book.

REPLICATE

Replicates control files to those locations specified by the *control_files* initialization parameter. Must be executed from within the RUN command.

Syntax

```
REPLICATE CONTROLFILE FROM 'filename';
```

REPORT

Provides detailed reports on database backup activity. These reports can provide information on backups that:

- Are required for restoration
- Require a specified number of incremental backups for restoration
- May be considered for obsolescence

REPORT can also display those datafiles that require the application of a specified number of days worth of archived redo log files in order to recover.

Oracle9i syntax

```
REPORT
{ { NEED BACKUP [ { INCREMENTAL | DAYS } [=] integer
                  | REDUNDANCY [=] integer
                  | RECOVERY WINDOW OF integer DAYS)
                  ]
  | UNRECOVERABLE
  }
  reportObject
| SCHEMA [atClause]
| OBSOLETE [obsoleteOpersList]
```

```
}
[ DEVICE TYPE deviceSpecifier [, deviceSpecifier ...];

reportObject :=
[ DATAFILE datafileSpec [, datafileSpec]...
| TABLESPACE [']tablespace_name[']
  [, [']tablespace_name['] ...]
| DATABASE [SKIP TABLESPACE
  [']tablespace_name['] [, [']tablespace_name[']]...]
]

atClause :=
{ AT TIME [=] 'date_string'
| AT SCN [=] integer
| AT SEQUENCE [=] integer THREAD [=] integer
}
```

Oracle8i syntax

```
REPORT
{ { NEED BACKUP [ { INCREMENTAL | DAYS } [=] integer
                 | REDUNDANCY [=] integer ]
  | UNRECOVERABLE
  }
  reportObject
| SCHEMA [atClause]
| OBSOLETE [obsoleteOpersList]
}

atClause :=
{ AT TIME [=] 'date_string'
| AT SCN [=] integer
| AT LOGSEQ [=] integer THREAD [=] integer
}
```

Keywords

NEED BACKUP

   Reports on datafiles that require a backup based on a redundancy factor, incremental level, or recovery window

UNRECOVERABLE

   Reports on all unrecoverable datafiles

SCHEMA [atClause]
Reports on tablespaces and datafiles at a specific point in time

OBSOLETE [obsoleteOpersList]
Displays backups and copies that are no longer required and therefore can be removed

Examples

To report on those datafiles that, if restored, would require application of two days (or more) worth of archived redo log files:

```
RMAN> report need backup days 2 database;
```

To generate the same report but only for SYSTEM tablespace datafiles:

```
RMAN> report need backup days 2 tablespace system;
```

To list backups considered obsolete:

```
RMAN> report obsolete;
```

RESET DATABASE

Either creates a new incarnation of the target database, or resets the target database to a previous incarnation within the recovery catalog. This command is needed only when the target database has been opened with the *reset logs* option of the SQL ALTER DATABASE command. If you use the RMAN ALTER DATABASE command to reset logs, the target database is automatically reset within the catalog.

Syntax

```
RESET DATABASE [TO INCARNATION incarnation_key];
```

Keywords

INCARNATION incarnation_key
Specifies that an older incarnation of the database should be the current incarnation

RESTORE

Restores an entire backup, or a component of a backup, to the target database. For Oracle8i, this command must be executed from within the RUN command.

Oracle9i syntax

```
RESTORE
[(] restoreObject [(restoreSpecOperand
[restoreSpecOperand]...] [)]
[(] restoreObject [(restoreSpecOperand
[restoreSpecOperand]...] [)]...
[ CHANNEL [']channel_id[']
| PARMS [=] 'channel_parms'
| FROM { BACKUPSET | DATAFILECOPY }
| untilClause
| FROM TAG [=] [']tag_name[']
| VALIDATE
| CHECK LOGICAL
| CHECK READONLY
| DEVICE TYPE deviceSpecifier [, deviceSpecifier ...]
| FORCE
]
[ CHANNEL [']channel_id[']
| PARMS [=] 'channel_parms'
| FROM { BACKUPSET | DATAFILECOPY }
| untilClause
| FROM TAG [=] [']tag_name[']
| VALIDATE
| CHECK LOGICAL
| CHECK READONLY
| DEVICE TYPE deviceSpecifier [, deviceSpecifier ...]
| FORCE
]...;

restoreObject :=
{ CONTROLFILE [TO 'filename']
| DATABASE
  [SKIP [FOREVER] TABLESPACE
   [']tablespace_name['] [, [']tablespace_name['] ...]
  ]
| DATAFILE datafileSpec [, datafileSpec ...]
| TABLESPACE [']tablespace_name[']
   [, [']tablespace_name[']]...
```

```
| archivelogRecordSpecifier
}

restoreSpecOperand :=
{ CHANNEL [']channel_id[']
| FROM TAG [=] [']tag_name[']
| PARMS [=] 'channel_parms'
| FROM
  { AUTOBACKUP
    [{ MAXSEQ | MAXDAYS } [=] integer)
    [{ MAXSEQ | MAXDAYS } [=] integer) ...]
  | 'media_handle'
  }
}
```

Oracle8i syntax

```
RESTORE
[(] restoreObject [(restoreSpecOperand
[restoreSpecOperand]...] )]
[(] restoreObject [(restoreSpecOperand
[restoreSpecOperand]...] )]...
[ CHANNEL [']channel_id[']
| PARMS [=] 'channel_parms'
| FROM { BACKUPSET | DATAFILECOPY }
| untilClause
| FROM TAG [=] [']tag_name[']
| VALIDATE
| CHECK LOGICAL
| CHECK READONLY
]
[ CHANNEL [']channel_id[']
| PARMS [=] 'channel_parms'
| FROM { BACKUPSET | DATAFILECOPY }
| untilClause
| FROM TAG [=] [']tag_name[']
| VALIDATE
| CHECK LOGICAL
| CHECK READONLY
]...;

restoreSpecOperand :=
{ CHANNEL [']channel_id[']
| FROM TAG [=] [']tag_name[']
| PARMS [=] 'channel_parms'
}
```

Examples

Please see the earlier section "Restoring Files" for examples.

RESYNC

Resynchronizes the catalog with the control files of the target database. For example, you use RESYNC when the recovery catalog has been down for maintenance or other reasons, and needs to be synchronized with the target database. In general, most RMAN operations synchronize the catalog with the target database. For Oracle8*i*, this command must be executed from within the RUN command.

Syntax

```
RESYNC CATALOG [FROM CONTROLFILECOPY 'filename'];
```

RUN

Executes a series of commands. With Oracle8*i*, certain commands such as BACKUP and RESTORE are required to be executed within the braces of the RUN command. In many cases, that requirement has been removed with Oracle9*i*. However, even with Oracle9*i*, there are still a few commands that must be executed from within the braces of RUN:

- ALLOCATE CHANNEL
- EXCUTE SCRIPT
- REPLICATE
- SWITCH

Syntax

```
RUN
{
    commands
}
```

SEND

Sends vendor-specific commands to one or more channels when using a media management layer. For Oracle8*i*, this command must be executed from within the RUN command.

Syntax

```
SEND
[ DEVICE TYPE deviceSpecifier [, deviceSpecifier]...]
| CHANNEL [']channel_id['] [, [']channel_id['] ...]
]
'command' [PARMS [=] 'channel_parms'];
```

SET

Establishes settings for the current RMAN session. The settings terminate with the RMAN session.

Oracle9i syntax

```
SET { setRmanOtion [;] | setRunOption; }

setRmanOption :=
{ ECHO { ON | OFF }
| DBID [=] integer
| CONTROLFILE AUTOBACKUP FORMAT
  FOR DEVICE TYPE deviceSpecifier TO 'format_string' }

setRunOption :=
{ NEWNAME FOR DATAFILE datafileSpec TO { 'filename' | NEW
}
| MAXCORRUPT FOR DATAFILE datafileSpec
  [, datafileSpec ...] TO integer
| ARCHIVELOG DESTINATION TO 'log_archive_dest'
| untilClause
| BACKUP COPIES [=] integer
| COMMAND ID TO 'string'
| AUTOLOCATE { ON | OFF }
| CONTROLFILE AUTOBACKUP
  FORMAT FOR DEVICE TYPE deviceSpecifier TO
      'format_string'
}
```

Oracle8i syntax

```
SET { setRmanOption [;] | setRunOption;}

setRmanOption :=
 { AUXNAME FOR DATAFILE datafileSpec TO { 'filename' |
     NULL }
   | DBID [=] integer
   | SNAPSHOT CONTROLFILE NAME TO 'filename'
   }
 | ECHO { ON | OFF }
 };

setRunOption :=
{ { NEWNAME FOR DATAFILE datafileSpec TO 'filename'
  | MAXCORRUPT FOR DATAFILE datafileSpec
     [, datafileSpec ...]
    TO integer
  | ARCHIVELOG DESTINATION TO 'log_archive_dest'
  | untilClause
  | DUPLEX [=] { ON | OFF | integer }
  | COMMAND ID TO 'string'
  | AUTOLOCATE { ON | OFF }
  }
| LIMIT CHANNEL ['] channel_id [']
  limitOptions [limitOptions ...]
}

limitOptions :=
{ KBYTES [=] integer
| READRATE [=] integer
| MAXOPENFILES [=] integer
}
```

Example

The following example, which does a complete database backup,
uses the SET command to establish a limit on channel *d1*. The
limit ensures that any backup piece created through this channel
will be less than or equal to 1.9 MB.

```
RMAN> run {
2> allocate channel d1 type disk;
3> set limit channel d1 kbytes 1900000;
4> backup format='d99/backups/%U' archivelog all delete
5> input;}
```

SHOW (Oracle9i only)

Displays current settings established with the CONFIGURE command.

Syntax

```
SHOW
{ RETENTION POLICY
| [DEFAULT] DEVICE TYPE
| [AUXILIARY] CHANNEL [FOR DEVICE TYPE deviceSpecifier]
| MAXSETSIZE
| { DATAFILE | ARCHIVELOG } BACKUP COPIES
| BACKUP OPTIMIZATION
| SNAPSHOT CONTROLFILE NAME
| AUXNAME
| EXCLUDE
| CONTROLFILE AUTOBACKUP [FORMAT]
| ALL
};
```

SHUTDOWN

Shuts down the target database.

Syntax

```
SHUTDOWN [ NORMAL | ABORT | IMMEDIATE | TRANSACTIONAL ][;]
```

SPOOL (Oracle9i only)

Causes output generated from RMAN to be written to a log file.

Syntax

```
SPOOL LOG { OFF | TO filename } [APPEND][;]
```

SQL

Allows you to execute SQL commands from the RMAN prompt.

Syntax

```
SQL {' | "}command{' | "};
```

Examples

The following example uses SQL to issue an ALTER SYSTEM command:

```
RMAN> SQL 'alter system switch logfile';
```

This next example, which takes a datafile offline, illustrates the use of an SQL command that has ticks within it. Each occurrence of two ticks in the string results in one tick in the command as actually executed.

```
RMAN> SQL "alter database datafile
   ''/d01/oradata/brdstn/users_01.dbf'' offline";
```

STARTUP

Starts a target database from within RMAN. This command is analogous to the SQL STARTUP command.

Syntax

```
STARTUP
[ FORCE
| { NOMOUNT | MOUNT }
| DBA
| PFILE [=] [']filename[']
]
[ FORCE
| { NOMOUNT | MOUNT }
| DBA
| PFILE [=] [']filename[']
]... [;]
```

SWITCH

This command is analogous to the SQL ALTER DATABASE RENAME *file* command. It specifies that a datafile copy is now the current datafile and must be run from within the RUN command.

Syntax

```
SWITCH
{ DATAFILE datafileSpec
  [ TO DATAFILECOPY { 'filename' | TAG [=] [']tag_name['] 
}]
| DATAFILE ALL
};
```

Example

The following example copies the datafile for the USERS tablespace to a different location. After doing so, the SWITCH command modifies the control file to make the datafile copy the current datafile.

```
RMAN> sql "alter database datafile
  ''/d02/oradata/brdstn/users_01.dbf'' offline";
RMAN> sql statement: alter database datafile
2> ''/d02/oradata/brdstn/users_01.dbf'' offline
RMAN> run {
2> copy datafile '/d02/oradata/brdstn/users_01.dbf'
3> to '/d03/oradata/brdstn/users_01.dbf';
4> switch datafile '/d02/oradata/brdstn/users_01.dbf'
5> to datafilecopy '/d03/oradata/brdstn/users_01.dbf';
6> }

Starting copy at 10-JUL-01
allocated channel: ORA_DISK_1
channel ORA_DISK_1: copied datafile 6
output filename=/d03/oradata/brdstn/users_01.dbf recid=4
  stamp=434740922
Finished copy at 10-JUL-01

datafile 6 switched to datafile copy
input datafilecopy recid=4 stamp=434740922 filename=/d03/
  oradata/brdstn/users_01.dbf

RMAN> recover datafile '/d03/oradata/brdstn/users_01.dbf';

Starting recover at 10-JUL-01
using channel ORA_DISK_1

starting media recovery
media recovery complete
```

```
Finished recover at 10-JUL-01

RMAN> sql "alter database datafile
   ''/d03/oradata/brdstn/foo_01.dbf'' online";

sql statement: alter database datafile
   ''/d03/oradata/brdstn/users_01.dbf'' online
```

untilClause

A subclause, used by various RMAN commands, to specify an
upper limit for time, SCN, or log sequence numbers.

Syntax

```
UntilClause :=
{ UNTIL TIME [=] 'date_string'
| UNTIL SCN [=] integer
| UNTIL SEQUENCE [=] integer THREAD [=] integer
}
```

UPGRADE CATALOG

Upgrades a recovery catalog schema to a newer version that is
required by the RMAN executable. You cannot use an RMAN
binary against a catalog that was created with a lesser version. For
example, you cannot use an Oracle 9.0.1 RMAN binary to
connect to an Oracle 8.1.7 catalog.

Syntax

```
UPGRADE CATALOG [TABLESPACE [']tablespace_name[']] [;]
```

VALIDATE

Checks the integrity of a backup. All the associated backup pieces
are examined to determine whether their contents can be restored
if necessary and if they are free of physical corruption. For
Oracle8i, this command must be executed from within the RUN
command.

Oracle9i syntax

```
VALIDATE BACKUPSET primary_key [, primary_key ...]
[ CHECK LOGICAL
| DEVICE TYPE deviceSpecifier [, deviceSpecifier ...]
]
[ CHECK LOGICAL
| DEVICE TYPE deviceSpecifier [, deviceSpecifier ...]
]...;
```

Oracle8i syntax

```
VALIDATE BACKUPSET primary_key [, primary_key ...]
[ CHECK LOGICAL ];
```

Example

The following example uses the VALIDATE command to validate
backup set number 41. The resulting output indicates whether the
backup set can be restored.

```
RMAN> run {
2> allocate channel d1 type disk;
3> validate backupset 21;
4> }

released channel: ORA_DISK_1
allocated channel: d1
channel d1: sid=17 devtype=DISK

channel d1: starting validation of datafile backupset
channel d1: restored backup piece 1
piece handle=/d0999/rman_0ncuja8a_1_1.bus tag=null
params=NULL
channel d1: validation complete
released channel: d1
```

Other Titles Available from O'Reilly

Oracle SQL*Plus: The Definitive Guide

By Jonathan Gennick
1st Edition March 1999
526 pages, ISBN 1-56592-578-5

This book is the definitive guide to SQL*Plus, Oracle's interactive query tool. Despite the wide availability and usage of SQL*Plus, few developers and DBAs know how powerful it really is. This book introduces SQL*Plus, provides a syntax quick reference, and describes how to write and execute script files, generate ad hoc reports, extract data from the database, query the data dictionary tables, use the SQL*Plus administrative features (new in Oracle8i), and much more.

Oracle Essentials: Oracle9i, Oracle8i & Oracle8

By Rick Greenwald, Robert Stackowiak & Jonathan Stern
2nd Edition June 2001
381 pages, ISBN 0-596-00179-7

Updated for Oracle's latest release, Oracle9i, *Oracle Essentials* is a concise and readable technical introduction to Oracle features and technologies, including the Oracle architecture, data structures, configuration, networking, tuning, and data warehousing. It introduces such major Oracle9i features as Real Application clusters, flashback queries, clickstream intelligence, Oracle Database and Web Cache, XML integration, the Oracle9i Application Server, Oracle9i Portal, and much more.

Oracle Database Administration: The Essential Reference

By David Kreines & Brian Laskey
1st Edition April 1999
580 pages, ISBN 1-56592-516-5

This book provides a concise reference to the enormous store of information Oracle8 or Oracle7 DBAs need every day. It covers DBA tasks (e.g., installation, tuning, backups, networking, auditing, query optimization) and provides quick references to initialization parameters, SQL statements, data dictionary tables, system privileges, roles, and syntax for SQL*Plus, Export, Import, and SQL*Loader.

Oracle DBA Checklists Pocket Reference

By Quest Software
1st Edition April 2001
80 pages, ISBN 0-596-00122-3

In a series of easy-to-use checklists, the *Oracle DBA Checklists Pocket Reference* summarizes the enormous number of tasks an Oracle DBA must perform. Each section takes the stress out of DBA problem solving with a step-by-step "cookbook" approach to presenting DBA quick-reference material, making it easy to find the information you need—and find it fast.

O'REILLY®

Java Programming with Oracle JDBC

By Donald K. Bales
1st Edition December 2001
496 pages, ISBN 0-596-00088-X

Learn how to leverage JDBC, a key Java technology used to access relational data from Java programs, in an Oracle environment. Author Don Bales begins by teaching you the mysteries of establishing database connections, and how to issue SQL queries and get results back. You'll move on to advanced topics such as streaming large objects, calling PL/SQL procedures, and working with Oracle9i's object-oriented features, then finish with a look at transactions, concurrency management, and performance.

Building Oracle XML Applications

By Steve Muench
1st Edition September 2000
810 pages, Includes CD-ROM
ISBN 1-56592-691-9

Building Oracle XML Applications gives Java and PL/SQL developers a rich and detailed look at the many tools Oracle provides to support XML development. It shows how to combine the power of XML and XSLT with the speed, functionality, and reliability of the Oracle database. The author delivers nearly 800 pages of entertaining text, helpful and timesaving hints, and extensive examples that developers can put to use immediately to build custom XML applications. The accompanying CD-ROM contains JDeveloper 3.1, an integrated development environment for Java developers.

Unix for Oracle DBAs Pocket Reference

By Donald K. Burleson
1st Edition January 2001
110 pages, ISBN 0-596-00066-9

If you are an Oracle DBA moving to Unix from another environment such as Windows NT or IBM Mainframe, you know that the commands you need to learn are far different from those covered in most beginning Unix books. In this handy pocket-sized book, Don Burleson introduces those Unix commands that you as an Oracle DBA most need to know.

Perl for Oracle DBAs

By Andy Duncan & Jared Still
1st Edition August 2002
624 pages, ISBN 0-596-00210-6

Perl is a very helpful tool for Oracle database administrators, but too few DBAs realize how powerful Perl can be. *Perl for Oracle DBAs* describes what DBAs need to know about Perl and explains how they can use this popular open source language to manage, monitor, and tune their Oracle databases. The book also describes the Oracle/Perl software modules that tie these two environments together—for example, Oracle Call Interface (OCI), Perl DataBase Interface (DBI), DBD-Oracle, and mod_perl, etc. The book comes with a toolkit containing more than 100 ready-to-use programs that DBAs can put to immediate use in their Linux or Windows systems.

O'REILLY®

To order: *800-998-9938* • *order@oreilly.com* • *www.oreilly.com*
Online editions of most O'Reilly titles are available by subscription at *safari.oreilly.com*
Also available at most retail and online bookstores.

TOAD Pocket Reference for Oracle

By Jim McDaniel & Patrick McGrath
1st Edition August 2002
128 pages, ISBN 0-596-00337-4

This handy little book provides
database developers and administrators with quick access to TOAD feature summaries, hot keys,
productivity tips and tricks, and
much more. A perfect pocket-sized
guide that's easy to take anywhere,
TOAD Pocket Reference for Oracle
focuses on the major TOAD components, including the SQL Editor,
Data Grid, Schema Browser, SQL
Tuning module, and DBA tools (for
database administration, user
administration, and database performance).

O'REILLY®